MW01620441

Love Poems

of

ELIZABETH BARRETT BROWNING

and

ROBERT BROWNING

Selected, and with a Foreword, by

LOUIS UNTERMEYER

This edition published by Barnes & Noble, Inc.
by arrangement with Rutgers University Press and
by arrangement with the Estate of Louis Untermeyer,
Norma Anchin Untermeyer c/o Professional Publishing Services.
This edition was reprinted with expressed permission by Laurence S. Untermeyer.

1994 Barnes & Noble Books

ISBN 1-5661-9807-0 *paperback*
ISBN 1-5661-9688-4 *casebound*
ISBN 0-7607-2708-2 *gift edition*

Printed and bound in the United States of America

01 02 03 04 05 MP 12 11 10 9 8 7 6 5
01 02 03 04 05 MC 13 12 11 10 9 8 7
01 02 03 04 05 MGE 8 7 6 5 4 3 2 1

FG

Contents

LOVE POEMS OF ROBERT BROWNING

A Foreword

THE STORY of the Brownings is one of the strangest love stories of literature. Elizabeth Barrett was a thirty-nine-year-old invalid when Robert Browning, six years younger than she, stormed impetuously into her life. She was already a well-known author; he was a rising but scarcely recognized poet.

Born in Durham, March 6, 1806, the eldest of eleven children, Elizabeth was extraordinarily precocious. She read Greek at eight; at twelve she wrote an "epic" in four books, *The Battle of Marathon,* which her father had printed. At fifteen she injured her spine, either by a fall from a horse or by a strain caused by tightening the saddle girths. A persistent cough kept her confined in London with occasional visits to the seashore. The death of a beloved brother by drowning and her father's jealous possessiveness plunged her into a half real, half-enforced melancholy. Approaching her forties, she seemed destined for a life of shrouded invalidism.

Her father, Edward Moulton Barrett, has been pictured as a cruel and almost tyrannical parent. Besier's popular play, *The Barretts of Wimpole Street,* presents him in the light of a villain, violent and even vindictive, a man from whom his children shrank in fear and who commanded their obedience but not their love. The disciples of Freud have made much of a subconscious incestuous attachment and have rung changes on the paradox of fascination and fear, of loving and loathing. But Elizabeth, Barrett's oldest child and his favorite daughter, was not, as we might be led to believe, revolted by her father's love. She returned his affection not only with the unreckoning simplicity of a child but with the full understanding of a constant companion. A collection of her poems carried this straightforward tribute:

DEDICATION

To My Father

WHEN your eyes fall upon this page of dedication, and you start to see to whom it is inscribed, your first thought will be of the time far off when I was a child and wrote verses, and when I dedicated them to you, who were my public and my critic. Of all that such a recollection implies of saddest and sweetest to both of us, it would become neither of us to speak before the world: nor would it be possible for us to speak of it to one another, with voices that did not falter. Enough, that what is in my heart when I write thus, will be fully known to yours.

And my desire is that *you,* who are a witness how if this art of poetry had been a less earnest object to me, it must have fallen from exhausted hands before this day,—that *you,* who have shared with me in things bitter and sweet, softening or enhancing them every day—that *you,* who hold with me over all sense of loss and transiency, one hope by one Name,—may accept the inscription of these volumes, the exponents of a few years of an existence which has been sustained and comforted by you as well as given. Somewhat more fainthearted than I used to be, it is my fancy thus to seem to return to a visible personal dependence on you, as if indeed I were a child again; to conjure your beloved image between myself and the public, so as to be sure of one smile,—and to satisfy my heart while I sanctify my ambition, by associating with the great pursuit of my life, its tenderest and holiest affection.

Your

E. B. B.

It might be surmised that this dedication was a youthful *quid pro quo*, the filial repayment of a girl just out of her teens. But this is far from chronological fact. The volume that contained this acknowledgment of glad dependence, loyalty and admiration was published in 1844, when Elizabeth Barrett was thirty-eight years old.

Just a year later Robert Browning was brought to her home. He was already in love with her, even before he saw her. She had praised some of his lines in a poem, "Lady Geraldine's Courtship," and his first letter to her began, "I love your verses with all my heart, dear Miss Barrett." Then, after a page or two of literary compliments, he added boyishly, "And I love you too." In spite of her father's disapproval, the young poet practically forced his way into the forbidding house, courted Elizabeth swiftly and tempestuously, and challenged the very authority of her father. To counteract Browning's growing influence, Mr. Barrett made plans to move the entire family to the country. Browning was now aroused to act; on September 12, 1846, he persuaded Elizabeth to slip from the house and marry him secretly in Marylebone Church. A week later, accompanied only by her maid Wilson and her dog Flush—the pet spaniel given to her by her friend Mary Russell Mitford, author of *Our Village*—the married poets crossed the channel, passed to Paris, to Pisa, and finally to Florence where they began a new life.

II

IN ITALY Mrs. Browning made an almost miraculous recovery. In spite of a frail body, she grew almost robust; at forty-three she gave birth to a son. Husband and wife luxuriated in a climate which gave them energy as well as happiness. Theirs was a long and industrious idyl.

Although the body of her work is scholarly to the point of solemnity, it is enlivened by wit and warmed by a pervasive sentiment. Time and again she gives us glimpses of her youth and its surroundings. Her poem "The Pet-Name" tells of a diminutive given to her in childhood by her brother, although the name itself (the contraction "Ba") is never given. She was a tiny person; "I am little, and like little things," she said, referring to her collection of miniature books, and she retained her fondness for the abbreviated pet-name throughout her life. When Browning used it after their marriage, she wrote, "I am glad you do not despise my own name too much, because I never was called Elizabeth by anyone who loved me at all." She enlarged upon the theme in sonnet XXXIII in *Sonnets from the Portuguese.*

The Pet-Name

——the name
Which from THEIR lips seemed a caress.
MISS MITFORD'S *Dramatic Scenes.*

I HAVE a name, a little name,
Uncadenced for the ear,
Unhonored by ancestral claim,
Unsanctified by prayer and psalm
The solemn font anear.

It never did to pages wove
For gay romance, belong.
It never dedicate did move
As "Sacharissa," unto love—
"Orinda," unto song.

Though I write books, it will be read
Upon the leaves of none,
And afterward, when I am dead,
Will ne'er be graved for sight or tread
Across my funeral stone.

This name, whoever chance to call,
Perhaps your smile may win.
Nay, do not smile! mine eyelids fall
Over mine eyes, and feel withal
The sudden tears within.

Is there a leaf that greenly grows
Where summer meadows bloom
But gathereth the winter snows,
And changeth to the hue of those,
If lasting till they come?

Is there a word, or jest, or game,
  But time encrusteth round
With sad associate thoughts the same?
And so to me my very name
  Assumes a mournful sound.

My brother gave that name to me
  When we were children twain;
When names acquired baptismally
Were hard to utter as to see
  That life had any pain.

No shade was on us then, save one
  Of chestnuts from the hill—
And through the word our laugh did run
As part thereof. The mirth being done,
  He calls me by it still.

Nay, do not smile! I hear in it
  What none of you can hear!
The talk upon the willow seat,
The bird and wind that did repeat
  Around, our human cheer.

I hear the birthday's noisy bliss,
  My sister's woodland glee,—
My father's praise, I did not miss,
When stooping down he cared to kiss
  The poet at his knee;—

And voices, which to name me, aye
  Their tenderest tones were keeping!—
To some I never more can say
An answer, till God wipes away
  In heaven those drops of weeping.

My name to me a sadness wears;
   No murmurs cross my mind;
Now God be thanked for these thick tears,
Which show, of those departed years,
   Sweet memories left behind!

Now God be thanked for years enwrought
   With love which softens yet!
Now God be thanked for every thought
Which is so tender it has caught
   Earth's guerdon of regret!

Earth saddens, never shall remove,
   Affections purely given;
And e'en that mortal grief shall prove
The immortality of love,
   And brighten it with Heaven.

III

FLUSH was an important member of the household. Never could Elizabeth forget his almost human devotion to her when she lay ill and weak and "he watched beside a bed—day and night unweary." "To Flush, My Dog" is a loving eulogy to a "gentle fellow-creature" and "sportive friend." As Elizabeth herself wrote in an unusually sprightly note: "The Flushes have their laurels as well as the Caesars—the chief difference (at least the very head and front of it) consisting, perhaps, in the bald head of the latter under the crown."

To Flush, My Dog

LOVING friend, the gift of one
Who her own true faith hath run,
  Through thy lower nature;
Be my benediction said
With my hand upon thy head,
  Gentle fellow-creature!

Like a lady's ringlets brown,
Flow thine silken ears adown
  Either side demurely
Of thy silver-suited breast
Shining out from all the rest
  Of thy body purely.

Darkly brown thy body is,
Till the sunshine striking this
  Alchemise its dullness;
When the sleek curls manifold
Flash all over into gold,
  With a burnished fulness.

Underneath my stroking hand,
Startled eyes of hazel bland
  Kindling, growing larger,
Up thou leapest with a spring,
Full of prank and curveting,
  Leaping like a charger.

Leap! thy broad tail waves a light;
Leap! thy slender feet are bright,
  Canopied in fringes.

Leap—those tasselled ears of thine
Flicker strangely, fair and fine,
Down their golden inches.

Yet, my pretty, sportive friend,
Little is't to such an end
That I praise thy rareness!
Other dogs may be thy peers
Haply in those drooping ears,
And this glossy fairness.

But of *thee* it shall be said,
This dog watched beside a bed
Day and night unweary,—
Watched within a curtained room,
Where no sunbeam brake the gloom
Round the sick and dreary.

Roses gathered for a vase,
In that chamber died apace,
Beam and breeze resigning—
This dog only, waited on,
Knowing that when light is gone,
Love remains for shining.

Other dogs in thymy dew
Tracked the hares and followed through
Sunny moor or meadow—
This dog only, crept and crept
Next a languid cheek that slept,
Sharing in the shadow.

Other dogs of loyal cheer
Bounded at the whistle clear,
Up the woodside hying—

This dog only, watched in reach
Of a faintly uttered speech,
  Or a louder sighing.

And if one or two quick tears
Dropped upon his glossy ears,
  Or a sigh came double,—
Up he sprang in eager haste,
Fawning, fondling, breathing fast,
  In a tender trouble.

And this dog was satisfied
If a pale thin hand would glide
  Down his dewlaps sloping,—
Which he pushed his nose within,
After,—platforming his chin
  On the palm left open.

This dog, if a friendly voice
Called him now to blither choice
  Than such a chamber-keeping,
"Come out!" praying from the door,—
Presseth backward as before,
  Up against me leaping.

Therefore to this dog will I,
Tenderly not scornfully,
  Render praise and favor:
With my hand upon his head,
Is my benediction said,
  Therefore, and forever.

And because he loves me so,
Better than his kind will do
  Often, man or woman,

Give I back more love again
Than dogs often take of men,
   Leaning from my Human.

Blessings on thee, dog of mine,
Pretty collars make thee fine,
   Sugared milk make fat thee!
Pleasures wag on in thy tail—
Hands of gentle motion fail
   Nevermore, to pat thee!

Downy pillow take thy head,
Silken coverlid bestead,
   Sunshine help thy sleeping!
No fly's buzzing wake thee up—
No man break thy purple cup,
   Set for drinking deep in.

Whiskered cats arointed flee—
Sturdy stoppers keep from thee
   Cologne distillations;
Nuts lie in thy path for stones,
And thy feast-day macaroons
   Turn to daily rations!

Mock I thee, in wishing weal?—
Tears are in my eyes to feel
   Thou art made so straightly,
Blessing needs must straighten too,—
Little canst thou joy or do,
   Thou who lovest *greatly*.

Yet be blessed to the height
Of all good and all delight
   Pervious to thy nature,

Only *loved* beyond that line,
With a love that answers thine,
Loving fellow-creature!

Often sentiment and humor are combined in a kind of mock-classicism. A sonnet entitled "Flush or Faunus" compares the golden-eyed little spaniel to the shaggy-coated god of the Arcadian woodlands. Mrs. Browning's mood had been a somber one, when suddenly a drooping ear flapped across her face to dry her tears and change sadness to pleased surprise.

Flush or Faunus

YOU see this dog. It was but yesterday
I mused forgetful of his presence here,
Till thought on thought drew downward tear on tear;
When from the pillow, where wet-cheeked I lay,
A head as hairy as Faunus, thrust its way
Right sudden against my face,—two golden-clear
Great eyes astonished mine,—a drooping ear
Did flap me on either cheek to dry the spray!
I started first, as some Arcadian,
Amazed by goatly god in twilight grove:
But as my bearded vision closelier ran
My tears off, I knew Flush, and rose above
Surprise and sadness; thanking the true Pan,
Who, by low creatures, leads to heights of love.

IV

THE FIXED devotion and unbroken compatibility of the Brownings is surprising when viewed in the light of the many differences in their backgrounds and temperaments. Although Mrs. Browning came from a large family, she was a delicate and always withdrawing introvert. Browning, on the other hand, though he had no brothers and only one sister, and was almost entirely privately educated, was a buoyant extrovert. Blessed with bounding health and a spirit which was not only happy but blindly optimistic, untroubled by financial worries, Browning was reared in comfort. He continued to live in an atmosphere of luxury and, after his marriage, in a growing expanse of affection. He and Elizabeth wrote with renewed fecundity. They grew deeply interested in Italian art and politics; intensities shared in common stimulated a richer poetry than either had hitherto created.

Their mutual love was accompanied by repeated tributes in verse. Besides the highly personal lyrics and dramatic monologues, Robert presented his wife with dozens of poems, objective and subjective, tracing the multiple variations and mutations of love. Upon completion of the richly detailed *Men and Women,* he added an "explanatory" poem entitled "One Word More" and dedicated it to his wife and co-worker. Part I of *The Ring and the Book* ends on a rhapsodic note which is a personal panegyric. It is so self-sufficing a passage—an unrhymed lyric—that it might be lifted from its context and entitled "To Elizabeth Barrett Browning, in Heaven."

O lyric Love, half angel and half bird,
And all a wonder and a wild desire,—
Boldest of hearts that ever braved the sun,
Took sanctuary within the holier blue,

And sang a kindred soul out to his face;—
Yet human at the red-ripe of the heart—
When the first summons from the darkling earth
Reached thee amid thy chambers, blanched their blue,
And bared them of the glory—to drop down,
To toil for man, to suffer or to die,—
This is the same voice: can thy soul know change?
Hail then, and hearken from the realms of help!
Never may I commence my song, my due
To God who best taught song by gift of thee,
Except with bent head and beseeching hand—
That still, despite the distance and the dark,
What was, again may be; some interchange
Of grace, some splendour once thy very thought,
Some benediction anciently thy smile:
—Never conclude, but raising hand and head
Thither where eyes, that cannot reach, yet yearn
For all hope, all sustainment, all reward,
Their utmost up and on,—so blessing back
In those thy realms of help, that heaven thy home,
Some whiteness which, I judge, thy face makes proud,
Some wanness where, I think, thy foot may fall!

V

ELIZABETH'S love was a combination of tenderness and veneration, humility and idolatry. Literature is rich in the outpouring of passion, but no woman had ever expressed her affection more warmly and more poignantly than Mrs. Browning's *Sonnets from the Portuguese*, forty-four interlocking poems which she had written secretly with no thought of publication. According to the English critic Edmund Gosse, who heard the story from Browning himself, the sonnets were made known to Browning in the following manner:

"Their custom was, Mr. Browning said, to write alone, and not to show each other what they had written. This was a rule which he sometimes broke through, but she never. He had the habit of working in a downstairs room, where their meals were spread, while Mrs. Browning studied in a room on the floor above. One day, early in 1847, their breakfast being over, Mrs. Browning went upstairs, while her husband stood at the window watching the street till the table should be cleared. He was presently aware of some one behind him, although the servant was gone. It was Mrs. Browning, who held him by the shoulder to prevent his turning to look at her, and at the same time pushed a packet of papers into the pocket of his coat. She told him to read that, and to tear it up if he did not like it; and then she fled again to her own room. Mr. Browning seated himself at the table and unfolded the parcel. It contained the series of sonnets which have now become so illustrious. As he read, his emotion and delight may be conceived. Before he had finished it was impossible for him to restrain himself . . . . he rushed upstairs, and stormed that guarded citadel. He was early conscious that these were treasures not to be kept from the world. 'I dared not reserve to myself,' he said, 'the finest sonnets written in any language since Shakespeare's.' "

The sonnets were highly personal; they were the very record and chronicle of Elizabeth's betrothal. Although her husband urged her to give them to the world, she was loth to consent to publication. Finally her friend, Mary

Russell Mitford, saw the series and persuaded their author to let her put them through the press.

The title was something of a mystery; it was a modest, and misleading, attempt to conceal the unimpeded confessions of an impassioned heart. The poems were obviously not translations; the title was merely one more token of domestic intimacy. At first Mrs. Browning suggested "Sonnets translated from the Bosnian." But the title finally chosen was another homage to Browning; it was an acknowledgment of her husband's playful way of calling her his "own little Portuguese" because of her olive skin.

VI

THE THEME of ecstatic love which swells throughout the *Sonnets from the Portuguese* is supplemented in "Life and Love," "Question and Answer," "Proof and Disproof," "A Denial," "Inclusions," and "Insufficiency." All of these are intensely intimate expressions of Elizabeth's emotions during her rapt meetings with Browning. He on his part returned her single devotion with unfaltering steadfastness.

Although Elizabeth lived until the age of fifty-five, Mr. Barrett never forgave her. He left her letters unopened; he forbade the family to mention her name. He nursed an intense and accumulating hurt. That she had become a wife and mother made no difference; to him she was always the wayward child who had not only defied him but wounded him deeply, a heartless and rebellious runaway.

Browning, her junior by six years, assumed the role of Elizabeth's father, as well as lover, husband, and companion. His strength made her strong; his confidence was her security. She lived in the light of his spirit, and literally died in his arms.

Long after her death, his eye caught a passage in *Life and Letters of Edward FitzGerald.* It was an unfortunate private opinion, written in a scurrilous vein, unlike the usual kindliness of the paraphraser of the Rubáiyát, but the editor had allowed it to be printed. "Mrs. Browning's death is rather a relief to me, I must say. No more *Aurora Leighs,* thank God. A woman of real genius, I know; but what is the upshot of it all! She and her sex had better mind the kitchen and her children, and perhaps the poor. Except in such things as little novels, they only devote themselves to what men do much better, leaving that which men do worse or not at all."

Although Mrs. Browning had been dead twenty-eight years, and FitzGerald himself was no longer alive, Browning's undying love flamed into anger and he wrote the following bitter retort:

To Edward FitzGerald

(1889)

I CHANCED upon a new book yesterday;
I opened it; and where my finger lay,
'Twixt page and uncut page, these words I read,—
Some six or seven, at most,—and learned thereby
That you, FitzGerald, whom by ear and eye
She never knew, thanked God my wife was dead.
Ay, dead, and were yourself alive, good Fitz,
How to return you thanks would task my wits.
Kicking you seems the common lot of curs,

While more appropriate greeting lends you grace;
Surely, to spit there glorifies your face,—
Spitting,—from lips once sanctified by hers.

Less personal than Mrs. Browning's, Robert Browning's love poems are not only more dramatic but more expansive in subject and far-reaching in effect. The very word "love" was often employed in a special sense; it was used to express the entire range of emotion, from body's hunger to spiritual passion, from tenderness for a particular woman to a universal concern for mankind. But it was also used to denote an aspiration toward the ultimate and a union with the absolute. It has been said that the cardinal doctrine of his gospel was condensed in two lines:

Let us say—not "Since we know, we love,"
But rather "Since we love, we know enough."

VII

THE POEMS in this volume are arranged not by chronology but by contrast. It is hoped that the reader will be held more by changes of mood and variety of meter than by an arrangement in the order of the poems' publication. Although the contents are stringently selected from a large body of verse, confined to one central emotion, the gamut ranges widely, from the perfect reciprocity of passion in "Love among the Ruins" to the unhappy resignation of "The Lost Mistress," from the feminine self-renunciation of "A Woman's Last Word," (and its half facetious, half ironic complement in Mrs. Browning's "A Man's Requirements") to the headlong fervor of "Meeting at Night."

Some of these poems are frankly personal and poignant; others are made up of dramatized, even over-theatricalized, emotions. But the very mixture, the union of subjective and objective lyrics and monologues, reflects the union of two great souls unforgettably revealed in their poetry.

Louis Untermeyer

Elizabeth Barrett Browning

Life and Love

I

FAST this Life of mine was dying,
  Blind already and calm as death,
Snowflakes on her bosom lying
  Scarcely heaving with her breath.

II

Love came by, and having known her
  In a dream of fabled lands,
Gently stooped, and laid upon her
  Mystic chrism of holy hands;

III

Drew his smile across her folded
  Eyelids, as the swallow dips;
Breathed as finely as the cold did
  Through the locking of her lips.

IV

So, when Life looked upward, being
  Warmed and breathed on from above,
What sight could she have for seeing,
  Evermore . . . . but only Love?

A Denial

I

WE have met late—it is too late to meet,
O friend, not more than friend!
Death's forecome shroud is tangled round my feet,
And if I step or stir, I touch the end.
In this last jeopardy
Can I approach thee, I, who cannot move?
How shall I answer thy request for love?
Look in my face and see.

II

I love thee not, I dare not love thee! Go
In silence; drop my hand.
If thou seek roses, seek them where they blow
In garden-alleys, not in desert-sand.
Can life and death agree,
That thou shouldst stoop thy song to my complaint?
I cannot love thee. If the word is faint,
Look in my face and see.

III

I might have loved thee in some former days.
Oh, then, my spirits had leapt
As now they sink, at hearing thy love-praise!
Before these faded cheeks were overwept,
Had this been asked of me,
To love thee with my whole strong heart and head,
I should have said still . . . . yes, but *smiled* and said,
"Look in my face and see!"

IV

But now . . . . God sees me, God, who took my heart
  And drowned it in life's surge.
In all your wide warm earth I have no part—
A light song overcomes me like a dirge.
  Could Love's great harmony
The saints keep step to when their bonds are loose,
Not weigh me down? am I a wife to choose?
  Look in my face and see—

V

While I behold, as plain as one who dreams,
  Some woman of full worth,
Whose voice, as cadenced as a silver stream's,
Shall prove the fountain-soul which sends it forth;
  One younger, more thought-free
And fair and gay, than I, thou must forget,
With brighter eyes than these . . . . which are not wet . . . .
  Look in my face and see!

VI

So farewell thou, whom I have known too late
  To let thee come so near.
Be counted happy while men call thee great,
And one belovèd woman feels thee dear!—
  Not I!—that cannot be.
I am lost, I am changed,—I must go farther, where
The change shall take me worse, and no one dare
  Look in my face and see.

VII

Meantime I bless thee. By these thoughts of mine
  I bless thee from all such!

I bless thy lamp to oil, thy cup to wine,
Thy hearth to joy, thy hand to an equal touch
　Of loyal troth. For me,
I love thee not, I love thee not! — away!
Here's no more courage in my soul to say
　"Look in my face and see."

Question and Answer

LOVE you seek for, presupposes
  Summer heat and sunny glow,
Tell me, do you find moss-roses
  Budding, blooming in the snow?
Snow might kill the rose-tree's root—
Shake it quickly from your foot,
  Lest it harm you as you go.

From the ivy where it dapples
  A grey ruin, stone by stone,
Do you look for grapes or apples,
  Or for sad green leaves alone?
Pluck the leaves off, two or three—
Keep them for morality
  When you shall be safe and gone.

Proof and Disproof

I

DOST thou love me, my Belovèd?
Who shall answer yes or no?
What is provèd or disprovèd
When my soul inquireth so,
Dost thou love me, my Belovèd?

II

I have seen thy heart to-day,
Never open to the crowd,
While to love me aye and aye
Was the vow as it was vowed
By thine eyes of steadfast grey.

III

Now I sit alone, alone—
And the hot tears break and burn,
Now, Belovèd, thou art gone,
Doubt and terror have their turn.
Is it love that I have known?

IV

I have known some bitter things,—
Anguish, anger, solitude.
Year by year an evil brings,
Year by year denies a good;
March winds violate my springs.

V

I have known how sickness bends,
I have known how sorrow breaks,—

How quick hopes have sudden ends,
   How the heart thinks till it aches
Of the smile of buried friends.

VI

Last, I have known *thee*, my brave
   Noble thinker, lover, doer!
The best knowledge last I have.
   But thou comest as the thrower
Of fresh flowers upon a grave.

VII

Count what feelings used to move me!
   Can this love assort with those?
Thou, who art so far above me,
   Wilt thou stoop so, for repose?
Is it true that thou canst love me?

VIII

Do not blame me if I doubt thee.
   I can call love by its name
When thine arm is wrapt about me;
   But even love seems not the same,
When I sit alone, without thee.

IX

In thy clear eyes I descried
   Many a proof of love, to-day;
But to-night, those unbelied
   Speechful eyes being gone away,
There's the proof to seek, beside.

X

Dost thou love me, my Belovèd?
Only *thou* canst answer yes!
And, thou gone, the proof's disprovèd,
And the cry rings answerless—
Dost thou love me, my Belovèd?

Inclusions

I

OH, wilt thou have my hand, Dear, to lie along in thine?
As a little stone in a running stream, it seems to lie and pine!
Now drop the poor pale hand, Dear, . . unfit to plight with thine.

II

Oh, wilt thou have my cheek, Dear, drawn closer to thine own?
My cheek is white, my cheek is worn, by many a tear run down.
Now leave a little space, Dear, . . lest it should wet thine own.

III

Oh, must thou have my soul, Dear, commingled with thy soul?—
Red grows the cheek, and warm the hand, . . the part is in the whole ! . .
Nor hands nor cheeks keep separate, when soul is joined to soul.

Insufficiency

I

THERE is no one beside thee, and no one above thee;
  Thou standest alone, as the nightingale sings!
  Yet my words that would praise thee are impotent things,
For none can express thee though all should approve thee!
I love thee so, Dear, that I only can love thee.

II

Say, what can I do for thee? . . weary thee . . grieve thee?
  Lean on my shoulder . . . new burdens to add?
  Weep my tears over thee . . making thee sad?
Oh, hold me not—love me not? let me retrieve thee!
I love thee so, Dear, that I only can leave thee.

A Valediction

GOD be with thee my beloved,—God be with thee!
  Else alone thou goest forth,
  Thy face unto the north,
Moor and pleasance all around thee and beneath thee
  Looking equal in one snow!
  While I who try to reach thee,
  Vainly follow, vainly follow,
  With the farewell and the hollo,
  And cannot reach thee so.
  Alas! I can but teach thee.
God be with thee my beloved,—God be with thee!

Can I teach thee, my beloved—can I teach thee?
  If I said, Go left or right,
  The counsel would be light,
The wisdom, poor of all that could enrich thee!
  My right would show like left;
  My raising would depress thee,
  My choice of light would blind thee,
  Of way, would leave behind thee,
  Of end, would leave bereft!
  Alas! I can but bless thee—
May God teach thee my beloved,—may God teach thee!

Can I bless thee, my beloved,—can I bless thee?
  What blessing word can I,
  From mine own tears, keep dry?
What flowers grow in my field wherewith to dress thee?
  My good reverts to ill;
  My calmnesses would move thee,

My softnesses would prick thee,
My bindings up would break thee,
My crownings, curse and kill.
Alas! I can but love thee.
May God bless thee my beloved,—may God bless thee!

Can I love thee, my beloved,—can I love thee?
And is *this* like love, to stand
With no help in my hand,
When strong as death I fain would watch above thee?
My love-kiss can deny
No tears that fall beneath it:
Mine oath of love can swear thee
From no ill that comes near thee,—
And thou diest while I breathe it,
And I—*I* can but die!
May God love thee my beloved,—may God love thee!

A Seaside Walk

I

WE walked beside the sea
After a day which perished silently
Of its own glory—like the Princess weird
Who, combating the Genius, scorched and seared,
Uttered with burning breath, "Ho! victory!"
And sank adown an heap of ashes pale.
So runs the Arab tale.

II

The sky above us showed
An universal and unmoving cloud,
On which the cliffs permitted us to see
Only the outline of their majesty,
As master minds, when gazed at by the crowd!
And, shining with a gloom, the water grey
Swang in its moon-taught way.

III

Nor moon, nor stars were out.
They did not dare to tread so soon about,
Though trembling, in the footsteps of the sun.
The light was neither night's nor day's, but one
Which, life-like, had a beauty in its doubt:
And Silence's impassioned breathings round
Seemed wandering into sound.

IV

O solemn-beating heart
Of nature! I have knowledge that thou art

Bound unto man's by cords he cannot sever—
And, what time they are slackened by him ever.
So to attest his own supernal part,
Still runneth thy vibration fast and strong,
The slackened cord along.

V

For though we never spoke
Of the grey water and the shaded rock,
Dark wave and stone unconsciously were fused
Into the plaintive speaking that we used
Of absent friends and memories unforsook;
And, had we seen each other's face, we had
Seen haply, each was sad.

Calls on the Heart

I

FREE Heart, that singest to-day
Like a bird on the first green spray,
Wilt thou go forth to the world,
Where the hawk hath his wing unfurled,
To follow, perhaps, thy way?
Where the tamer thine own will bind,
And, to make thee sing, will blind,
While the little hip grows for the free behind?
Heart, wilt thou go?
—"No, no!
Free hearts are better so."

II

The world, thou hast heard it told,
Has counted its robber-gold,
And the pieces stick to the hand:
The world goes riding it fair and grand,
While the truth is bought and sold:
World-voices east, world-voices west,
They call thee, Heart, from thine early rest,
"Come hither, come hither, and be our guest."
Heart, wilt thou go?
—"No, no!
Good hearts are calmer so."

III

Who calleth thee, Heart? World's Strife,
With a golden heft to his knife;

World's Mirth, with a finger fine
That draws on a board in wine
Her blood-red plans of life;
World's Gain, with a brow knit down;
World's Fame, with a laurel crown
Which rustles most as the leaves turn brown:
Heart, wilt thou go?
—"No, no!
Calm hearts are wiser so."

IV

Hast heard that Proserpina
(Once fooling) was snatched away
To partake the dark king's seat,
And the tears ran fast on her feet
To think how the sun shone yesterday?
With her ankles sunken in asphodel
She wept for the roses of earth which fell
From her lap when the wild car drave to hell.
Heart, wilt thou go?
—"No, no!
Wise hearts are warmer so."

V

And what is this place not seen,
Where hearts may hide serene?
" 'Tis a fair still house well kept,
Which humble thoughts have swept,
And holy prayers made clean.
There I sit with Love in the sun,
And we two never have done
Singing sweeter songs than are guessed by *one.*"

Heart, wilt thou go?
—"No, no!
Warm hearts are fuller so."

VI

O Heart, O Love, I fear
That love may be kept too near.
Hast heard, O heart, that tale,
How Love may be false and frail
To a heart once holden dear?
—"But this true love of mine
Clings fast as the clinging vine,
And mingles pure as the grapes in wine."
Heart, wilt thou go?
—"No, no!
Full hearts beat higher so."

VII

O Heart, O Love, beware!—
Look up, and boast not there.
For who has twirled at the pin?
'Tis the world, between Death and Sin,—
The world, and the world's Despair!
And Death has quickened his pace
To the hearth, with a mocking face,
Familiar as Love, in Love's own place—
Heart, wilt thou go?
"Still, no!
High hearts must grieve even so."

VIII

The house is waste to-day,—
The leaf has dropt from the spray,

The thorn, prickt through to the song:
If summer doeth no wrong
The winter will, they say.
Sing, Heart! what heart replies?
In vain we were calm and wise,
If the tears unkissed stand in our eyes.
Heart, wilt thou go?
—"Ah, no!
Grieved hearts must break even so."

IX

Howbeit all is not lost:
The warm noon ends in frost,
The worldly tongues of promise,
Like sheep-bells, die off from us
On the desert hills cloud-crossed!
Yet, through the silence, shall
Pierce the death-angel's call,
And "Come up hither," recover all.
Heart, wilt thou go?
—"I go!
Broken hearts triumph so."

Catarina to Camoens

(Dying in his absence abroad, and referring to the poem in which he recorded the sweetness of her eyes)

ON the door you will not enter,
I have gazed too long—adieu!
Hope withdraws her peradventure—
Death is near me,—and not *you!*
Come, O lover!
Close and cover
These poor eyes, you called, I ween,
"Sweetest eyes, were ever seen."

When I heard you sing that burden
In my vernal days and bowers,
Other praises disregarding,
I but hearkened that of yours,—
Only saying
In heart-playing,
"Blessed eyes mine eyes have been,
If the sweetest, *his* have seen!"

But all changes. At this vesper,
Cold the sun shines down the door.
If you stood there, would you whisper
"Love, I love you," as before,—
Death pervading
Now, and shading
Eyes you sang of, that yestreen,
As the sweetest ever seen?

Yes! I think, were you beside them,
  Near the bed I die upon,—
Though their beauty you denied them,
  As you stood there looking down,
    You would truly
    Call them duly,
For the love's sake found therein,—
"Sweetest eyes were ever seen."

And if *you* looked down upon them,
  And if *they* looked up to *you*,
All the light which has foregone them
  Would be gathered back anew!
    They would truly
    Be as duly
Love-transformed to Beauty's sheen,—
"Sweetest eyes, were ever seen."

But, ah me! you only see me
  In your thoughts of loving man,
Smiling soft perhaps and dreamy
  Through the wavings of my fan,—
    And unweeting
    Go repeating,
In your reverie serene,
"Sweetest eyes, were ever seen."

While my spirit leans and reaches
  From my body still and pale,
Fain to hear what tender speech is
  In your love to help my bale—
    O my poet
    Come and show it!

Come, of latest love to glean
"Sweetest eyes, were ever seen."

O my poet, O my prophet,
  When you praised their sweetness so,
Did you think, in singing of it,
  That it might be near to go?
    Had you fancies
    From their glances,
That the grave would quickly screen
"Sweetest eyes, were ever seen?"

No reply! The fountains warble
  In the court-yard sounds alone:
As the water to the marble
  So my heart falls with a moan,
    From love-sighing
    To this dying!
Death forerunneth Love, to win
"Sweetest eyes, were ever seen."

Will you come? when I'm departed
  Where all sweetnesses are hid—
When thy voice, my tender-hearted,
  Will not lift up either lid,
    Cry, O lover,
    Love is over!
Cry beneath the cypress green—
"Sweetest eyes, were ever seen."

When the angelus is ringing,
  Near the convent will you walk,

And recall the choral singing
Which brought angels down our talk?
Spirit-shriven
I viewed Heaven,
Till you smiled—"Is earth unclean,
Sweetest eyes, were ever seen?"

When beneath the palace-lattice,
You ride slow as you have done,
And you see a face there—*that* is
Not the old familiar one,—
Will you oftly
Murmur softly,
"Here, ye watched me morn and e'en,
Sweetest eyes, were ever seen!"

When the palace ladies sitting
Round your gittern, shall have said,
"Poet, sing those verses written
For the lady who is dead,"
Will you tremble,
Yet dissemble,—
Or sing hoarse, with tears between,
"Sweetest eyes, were ever seen?"

Sweetest eyes! How sweet in flowings,
The repeated cadence is!
Though you sang a hundred poems,
Still the best one would be this.
I can hear it
'Twixt my spirit

And the earth noise intervene—
"Sweetest eyes, were ever seen."

But the priest waits for the praying,
   And the choir are on their knees,
And the soul must pass away in
   Strains more solemn high than these!
      Miserere
      For the weary—
Oh, no longer for Catrine,
"Sweetest eyes, were ever seen!"

Keep my riband, take and keep it,
   I have loosed it from my hair;
Feeling, while you overweep it,
   Not alone in your despair,
      Since with saintly
      Watch, unfaintly,
Out of Heaven shall o'er you lean
"Sweetest eyes, were ever seen."

But—but *now*—yet unremoved
   Up to Heaven, they glisten fast:
You may cast away, Beloved,
   In your future all my past;
      Such old phrases
      May be praises
For some fairer bosom-queen—
"Sweetest eyes, were ever seen!"

Eyes of mine, what are ye doing?
   Faithless, faithless—praised amiss

If a tear be of your showing,
   Drop for any hope of *his!*
      Death hath boldness
      Besides coldness,
If unworthy tears demean
"Sweetest eyes, were ever seen."

I will look out to his future—
   I will bless it till it shine:
Should he ever be a suitor
   Unto sweeter eyes than mine,
      Sunshine gild them,
      Angels shield them,
Whatsoever eyes terrene
Be the sweetest *his* have seen!

A Dead Rose

OH rose! who dares to name thee?
No longer roseate now, nor soft, nor sweet;
But pale, and hard, and dry, as stubble wheat,—
Kept seven years in a drawer—thy titles shame thee.

The breeze that used to blow thee
Between the hedge-row thorns, and take away
An odor up the lane to last all day,—
If breathing now,—unsweetened would forego thee.

The sun that used to smite thee,
And mix his glory in thy gorgeous urn,
Till beam appeared to bloom, and flower to burn,—
If shining now,—with not a hue would light thee.

The dew that used to wet thee,
And, white first, grow incarnadined, because
It lay upon thee where the crimson was,—
If dropping now, would darken where it met thee.

The fly that lit upon thee,
To stretch the tendrils of his tiny feet,
Along thy leaf's pure edges, after heat,—
If lighting now, would coldly overrun thee.

The bee that once did suck thee,
And build thy perfumed ambers up his hive,
And swoon in thee for joy, till scarce alive,—
If passing now, would blindly overlook thee.

The heart doth recognize thee,
Alone, alone! The heart doth smell thee sweet,
Doth view thee fair, doth judge thee most complete—
Though seeing now those changes that disguise thee.

Yes, and the heart doth owe thee
More love, dead rose! than to such roses bold
As Julia wears at dances, smiling cold!—
Lie still upon this heart—which breaks below thee!

A Woman's Shortcomings

I

SHE has laughed as softly as if she sighed,
  She has counted six and over,
Of a purse well filled, and a heart well tried—
  Oh each a worthy lover!
They "give her time;" for her soul must slip
  Where the world has set the grooving:
She will lie to none with her fair red lip—
  But love seeks truer loving.

II

She trembles her fan in a sweetness dumb,
  As her thoughts were beyond recalling,
With a glance for *one,* and a glance for *some,*
  For her eyelids rising and falling;
Speaks common words with a blushful air,
  Hears bold words, unreproving;
But her silence says—what she never will swear—
  And love seeks better loving.

III

Go, lady, lean to the night-guitar,
  And drop a smile to the bringer,
Then smile as sweetly, when he is far,
  At the voice of an indoor singer.
Bask tenderly beneath tender eyes;
  Glance lightly on their removing;
And join new vows to old perjuries—
  But dare not call it loving.

IV

Unless you can think, when the song is done,
  No other is soft in the rhythm;
Unless you can feel, when left by one,
  That all men else go with him;
Unless you can know, when unpraised by his breath,
  That your beauty itself wants proving;
Unless you can swear, "For life, for death!"—
  Oh fear to call it loving!

V

Unless you can muse in a crowd all day,
  On the absent face that fixed you;
Unless you can love, as the angels may,
  With the breadth of heaven betwixt you;
Unless you can dream that his faith is fast,
  Through behoving and unbehoving;
Unless you can *die* when the dream is past—
  Oh never call it loving!

A Man's Requirements

I

LOVE me, sweet, with all thou art,
   Feeling, thinking, seeing,—
Love me in the lightest part,
   Love me in full being.

II

Love me with thine open youth
   In its frank surrender;
With the vowing of thy mouth,
   With its silence tender.

III

Love me with thine azure eyes,
   Made for earnest granting!
Taking color from the skies,
   Can Heaven's truth be wanting?

IV

Love me with their lids, that fall
   Snow-like at first meeting:
Love me with thine heart, that all
   The neighbors then see beating.

V

Love me with thine hand stretched out
   Freely—open-minded:
Love me with thy loitering foot,—
   Hearing one behind it.

VI

Love me with thy voice, that turns
  Sudden faint above me;
Love me with thy blush that burns
  When I murmur "Love me!"

VII

Love me with thy thinking soul—
  Break it to love-sighing;
Love me with thy thoughts that roll
  On through living—dying.

VIII

Love me in thy gorgeous airs,
  When the world has crowned thee!
Love me, kneeling at thy prayers,
  With the angels round thee.

IX

Love me pure, as musers do,
  Up the woodlands shady:
Love me gaily, fast, and true,
  As a winsome lady.

X

Through all hopes that keep us brave,
  Further off or nigher,
Love me for the house and grave,—
  And for something higher.

XI

Thus, if thou wilt prove me, dear,
    Woman's love no fable,
I will love *thee*—half-a-year—
    As a man is able.

My Heart and I

I

ENOUGH! we're tired, my heart and I.
  We sit beside the headstone thus,
  And wish that name were carved for us.
The moss reprints more tenderly
  The hard types of the mason's knife,
  As heaven's sweet life renews earth's life
With which we're tired, my heart and I.

II

You see we're tired, my heart and I.
  We dealt with books, we trusted men,
  And in our own blood drenched the pen,
As if such colors could not fly.
  We walked too straight for fortune's end,
  We loved too true to keep a friend:
At last we're tired, my heart and I.

III

How tired we feel, my heart and I!
  We seem of no use in the world;
  Our fancies hang grey and uncurled
About men's eyes indifferently;
  Our voice, which thrilled you so; will let
  You sleep; our tears are only wet:
What do we here, my heart and I?

IV

So tired, so tired, my heart and I!
  It was not thus in that old time
  When Ralph sat with me 'neath the lime

To watch the sunset from the sky.
"Dear love, you're looking tired," he said;
I, smiling at him, shook my head:
'Tis now we're tired, my heart and I.

V

So tired, so tired, my heart and I!
Though now none takes me on his arm
To fold me close, and kiss me warm
Till each quick breath end in a sigh
Of happy languor. Now, alone,
We lean upon this graveyard stone,
Uncheered, unkissed, my heart and I.

VI

Tired out we are, my heart and I.
Suppose the world brought diadems
To tempt us, crusted with loose gems
Of powers and pleasures? Let it try.
We scarcely care to look at even
A pretty child, or God's blue heaven,
We feel so tired, my heart and I.

VII

Yet who complains? My heart and I?
In this abundant earth no doubt
Is little room for things worn out:
Disdain them, break them, throw them by!
And if, before the days grew rough,
We *once* were loved, used,—well enough
I think we've fared, my heart and I.

A False Step

I

SWEET, thou hast trod on a heart.
  Pass; there's a world full of men;
And women as fair as thou art
  Must do such things now and then.

II

Thou only hast stepped unaware;
  Malice, not one can impute;
And why should a heart have been there,
  In the way of a fair woman's foot?

III

It was not a stone that could trip,
  Nor was it a thorn that could rend:
Put up thy proud underlip!
  'Twas merely the heart of a friend.

IV

And yet, peradventure, one day
  Thou, sitting alone at the glass,
Remarking the bloom gone away,
  Where the smile in its dimplement was,

V

And seeking around thee in vain,
  From hundreds who flattered before,
Such a word as, "Oh, not in the main
  Do I hold thee less precious, but more!" . . .

VI

Thou'lt sigh, very like, on thy part,
"Of all I have known or can know,
I wish I had only that heart
I trod upon ages ago!"

Loved Once

I

I CLASSED, appraising once,
Earth's lamentable sounds,—the welladay,
The jarring yea and nay,
The fall of kisses on unanswering clay,
The sobbed farewell, the welcome mournfuller;
But all did leaven the air
With a less bitter leaven of sure despair
Than these words, "I loved *once.*"

II

And who saith "I loved *once*"?
Not angels, whose clear eyes, love, love, foresee,
Love, through eternity,
And by *To Love* to apprehend *To Be.*
Not God, called *Love,* his noble crown-name casting
A light too broad for blasting:
The great God changing not from everlasting,
Saith never, "I loved *once.*"

III

Oh, never is "Loved *once*"
Thy word, thou Victim-Christ, misprizèd friend!
Thy cross and curse may rend,
But, having loved, thou lovest to the end.
This is man's saying,—man's: too weak to move
One spherèd star above,
Man desecrates the eternal God-word Love
By his No More and Once.

IV

How say ye, "We loved once,"
Blasphemers? Is your earth not cold enow,
Mourners, without that snow?
Ah, friends, and would ye wrong each other so?
And could ye say of some whose love is known,
Whose prayers have met your own,
Whose tears have fallen for you, whose smiles have shown
So long, "We loved them *once*"?

V

Could ye, "We loved her once,"
Say calm of me, sweet friends, when out of sight?
When hearts of better right
Stand in between me and your happy light?
Or when, as flowers kept too long in the shade,
Ye find my colors fade,
And all that is not love in me decayed?
Such words,—ye loved me *once*!

VI

Could ye, "We loved her once,"
Say cold of me when further put away
In earth's sepulchral clay,
When mute the lips which deprecate today?
Not so! not then—least then! When life is shriven,
And death's full joy is given,
Of those who sit and love you up in heaven,
Say not "We loved them once."

VII

Say never, ye loved *once*:
God is too near above, the grave, beneath,
And all our moments breathe
Too quick in mysteries of life and death
For such a word. The eternities avenge
Affections light of range.
There comes no change to justify that change,
Whatever comes,—Loved *once*!

VIII

And yet that same word *once*
Is humanly acceptive. Kings have said,
Shaking a discrowned head,
"We ruled once,"—dotards, "We once taught and led;"
Cripples once danced i' the vines; and bards approved
Were once by scornings moved:
But love strikes one hour—*love*! those *never* loved
Who dream that they loved *once*.

The Lady's "Yes"

I

"YES," I answered you last night;
  "No," this morning, sir, I say:
Colors seen by candle-light
  Will not look the same by day.

II

When the viols played their best,
  Lamps above, and laughs below,
Love me sounded like a jest,
  Fit for *yes*, or fit for *no*.

III

Call me false, or call me free,
  Vow, whatever light may shine,
No man on your face shall see
  Any grief for change on mine.

IV

Yet the sin is on us both;
  Time to dance is not to woo:
Wooing light makes fickle troth,
  Scorn of *me* recoils on *you*.

V

Learn to win a lady's faith
  Nobly, as the thing is high,
Bravely, as for life and death,
  With a loyal gravity.

VI

Lead her from the festive boards,
Point her to the starry skies;
Guard her by your truthful words
Pure from courtship's flatteries.

VII

By your truth she shall be true,
Ever true, as wives of yore;
And her "Yes" once said to you
Shall be *Yes* for evermore.

A Year's Spinning

I

HE listened at the porch that day,
To hear the wheel go on and on;
And then it stopped, ran back a way,
While through the door he brought the sun.
But now my spinning is all done.

II

He sate beside me, with an oath
That love ne'er ended, once begun:
I smiled, believing for us both
What was the truth for only one.
And now my spinning is all done.

III

My mother cursed me that I heard
A young man's wooing as I spun:
Thanks, cruel mother, for that word,
For I have since a harder known.
And now my spinning is all done.

IV

I thought—O God!—my first-born's cry
Both voices to mine ear would drown:
I listened in mine agony—
It was the *silence* made me groan.
And now my spinning is all done.

V

Bury me 'twixt my mother's grave,
(Who cursed me on her death-bed lone,)

And my dead baby's (God it save!)
  Who, not to bless me, would not moan.
  And now my spinning is all done.

VI

A stone upon my heart and head,
  But no name written on the stone:
Sweet neighbors, whisper low instead,
  "This sinner was a loving one—
  And now her spinning is all done."

VII

And let the door ajar remain,
  In case he should pass by anon,
And leave the wheel out very plain,
  That *he*, when passing in the sun,
  May see the spinning is all done.

Change upon Change

I

FIVE months ago the stream did flow,
  The lilies bloomed within the sedge,
And we were lingering to and fro
Where none will track thee in this snow,
  Along the stream, beside the hedge.
Ah, sweet, be free to love and go!
  For, if I do not hear thy foot,
  The frozen river is as mute,
  The flowers have dried down to the root:
  And why, since these be changed since May,
    Shouldst *thou* change less than *they*?

II

And slow, slow as the winter snow,
  The tears have drifted to mine eyes;
And my poor cheeks, five months ago
Set blushing at thy praises so,
  Put paleness on for a disguise.
Ah, sweet, be free to praise and go!
  For, if my face is turned too pale,
  It was thine oath that first did fail;
  It was thy love proved false and frail:
  And why, since these be changed enow,
  Should *I* change less than *thou*?

That Day

I

I STAND by the river where both of us stood,
And there is but one shadow to darken the flood;
And the path leading to it, where both used to pass,
Has the step of but one to take dew from the grass,—
One forlorn since that day.

II

The flowers of the margin are many to see;
None stoops at my bidding to pluck them for me.
The bird in the alder sings loudly and long:
My low sound of weeping disturbs not his song,
As thy vow did that day.

III

I stand by the river, I think of the vow;
Oh, calm as the place is, vow-breaker, be thou!
I leave the flower growing, the bird unreproved:
Would I trouble *thee* rather than *them,* my beloved,—
And my lover that day?

IV

Go, be sure of my love, by that treason forgiven;
Of my prayers, by the blessings they win thee from heaven;
Of my grief (guess the length of the sword by the sheath's)
By the silence of life, more pathetic than death's!
Go,—be clear of that day!

Weariness

MINE eyes are weary of surveying
The fairest things, too soon decaying;
Mine ears are weary of receiving
The kindest words—ah, past believing!
Weary my hope, of ebb and flow;
Weary my pulse, of tunes of woe:
My trusting heart is weariest!
I would—I would, I were at rest!

For *me*, can earth refuse to fade?
For *me*, can words be faithful made?
Will *my* embitter'd hope be sweet?
My pulse forego the human beat?
No! Darkness must consume mine eye
Silence, mine ear—hope cease—pulse die
And o'er mine heart a stone be press'd—
Or vain this,—"Would I were at rest!"

There is a land of rest deferr'd:
Nor eye hath seen, nor ear hath heard,
Nor Hope hath trod the precinct o'er;
For Hope beheld its hope no more!
There, human pulse forgets its tone
There, hearts may know as they are known!
Oh, for dove's wings, thou dwelling blest,
To fly to *thee*, and be at rest!

Stanzas

I MAY sing; but minstrel's singing
Ever ceaseth with his playing.
I may smile; but time is bringing
Thoughts for smiles to wear away in.
I may view thee, mutely loving;
But *shall* view thee so in dying!
I may sigh; but life's removing,
And with breathing endeth sighing!
Be it so!

When no song of mine comes near thee,
Will its memory fail to soften?
When no smile of mine can cheer thee,
Will thy smile be used as often?
When my looks the darkness boundeth,
Will thine own be lighted after?
When my sigh no longer soundeth,
Wilt thou list another's laughter?
Be it so!

Grief

I TELL you, hopeless grief is passionless—
That only men incredulous of despair,
Half-taught in anguish, through the midnight air
Beat upward to God's throne in loud access
Of shrieking and reproach. Full desertness
In souls as countries, lieth silent-bare
Under the blanching, vertical eye-glare
Of the absolute Heavens. Deep-hearted man, express
Grief for thy Dead in silence like to death;
Most like a monumental statue set
In everlasting watch and moveless wo,
Till itself crumble to the dust beneath.
Touch it: the marble eyelids are not wet—
If it could weep, it could arise and go.

Substitution

WHEN some beloved voice that was to you
Both sound and sweetness, faileth suddenly,
And silence against which you dare not cry,
Aches round you like a strong disease and new—
What hope? what help? what music will undo
That silence to your sense? Not friendship's sigh—
Nor reason's subtle count! Not melody
Of viols, nor of pipes that Faunus blew—
Not songs of poets, nor of nightingales,
Whose hearts leap upward through the cypress trees
To the clear moon; nor yet the spheric laws
Self-chanted,—nor the angel's sweet All hails,
Met in the smile of God. Nay, none of these.
Speak Thou, availing Christ!—and fill this pause.

Love

WE cannot live, except thus mutually
We alternate, aware or unaware,
The reflex act of life: and when we bear
Our virtue onward most impulsively,
Most full of invocation, and to be
Most instantly compellant, certes, there
We live most life, whoever breathes most air
And counts his dying years by sun and sea.
But when a soul, by choice and conscience, doth
Throw out her full force on another soul,
The conscience and the concentration both
Make mere life, Love. For Life in perfect whole
And aim consummated, is Love in sooth,
As nature's magnet-heat rounds pole with pole.

May's Love

I

YOU love all, you say,
  Round, beneath, above me:
Find me then some way
  Better than to love me,
Me, too, dearest May!

II

O world-kissing eyes
  Which the blue heavens melt to!
I, sad, overwise,
  Loathe the sweet looks dealt to
All things—men and flies.

III

You love all, you say:
  Therefore, Dear, abate me—
Just your love, I pray!
  Shut your eyes and hate me
Only *me*—fair May!

SONNETS
FROM THE PORTUGUESE

I

I THOUGHT once how Theocritus had sung
Of the sweet years, the dear and wished-for years,
Who each one in a gracious hand appears
To bear a gift for mortals, old or young:
And, as I mused it in his antique tongue,
I saw, in gradual vision through my tears,
The sweet, sad years, the melancholy years,
Those of my own life, who by turns had flung
A shadow across me. Straightway I was 'ware,
So weeping, how a mystic Shape did move
Behind me, and drew me backward by the hair;
And a voice said in mastery, while I strove,—
"Guess now who holds thee?"—"Death," I said. But, there,
The silver answer rang,—"Not Death, but Love."

II

BUT only three in all God's universe
Have heard this word thou hast said,—Himself, beside
Thee speaking, and me listening! and replied
One of us . . . *that* was God, . . . and laid the curse
So darkly on my eyelids, as to amerce
My sight from seeing thee,—that if I had died,
The deathweights, placed there, would have signified
Less absolute exclusion. "Nay" is worse
From God than from all others, O my friend!
Men could not part us with their worldly jars,
Nor the seas change us, nor the tempests bend;
Our hands would touch for all the mountain bars:
And, heaven being rolled between us at the end,
We should but vow the faster for the stars.

III

UNLIKE are we, unlike, O princely Heart!
Unlike our uses and our destinies.
Our ministering two angels look surprise
On one another, as they strike athwart
Their wings in passing. Thou, bethink thee, art
A quest for queens to social pageantries,
With gages from a hundred brighter eyes
Than tears even can make mine, to play thy part
Of chief musician. What hast *thou* to do
With looking from the lattice-lights at me,
A poor, tired, wandering singer, singing through
The dark, and leaning up a cypress tree?
The chrism is on thine head,—on mine, the dew,—
And Death must dig the level where these agree.

IV

THOU hast thy calling to some palace-floor,
Most gracious singer of high poems! where
The dancers will break footing, from the care
Of watching up thy pregnant lips for more.
And dost thou lift this house's latch too poor
For hand of thine? and canst thou think and bear
To let thy music drop here unaware
In folds of golden fulness at my door?
Look up and see the casement broken in,
The bats and owlets builders in the roof!
My cricket chirps against thy mandolin.
Hush, call no echo up in further proof
Of desolation! there's a voice within
That weeps . . . as thou must sing . . . alone, aloof.

V

I LIFT my heavy heart up solemnly,
As once Electra her sepulchral urn,
And, looking in thine eyes, I overturn
The ashes at thy feet. Behold and see
What a great heap of grief lay hid in me,
And how the red wild sparkles dimly burn
Through the ashen greyness. If thy foot in scorn
Could tread them out to darkness utterly,
It might be well perhaps. But if instead
Thou wait beside me for the wind to blow
The grey dust up, . . . those laurels on thine head
O my Belovèd, will not shield thee so,
That none of all the fires shall scorch and shred
The hair beneath. Stand farther off then! go.

VI

GO from me. Yet I feel that I shall stand
Henceforward in thy shadow. Nevermore
Alone upon the threshold of my door
Of individual life, I shall command
The uses of my soul, nor lift my hand
Serenely in the sunshine as before,
Without the sense of that which I forbore—
Thy touch upon the palm. The widest land
Doom takes to part us, leaves thy heart in mine
With pulses that beat double. What I do
And what I dream include thee, as the wine
Must taste of its own grapes. And when I sue
God for myself, He hears that name of thine,
And sees within my eyes the tears of two.

VII

THE face of all the world is changed, I think,
Since first I heard the footsteps of thy soul
Move still, oh, still, beside me, as they stole
Betwixt me and the dreadful outer brink
Of obvious death, where I, who thought to sink,
Was caught up into love, and taught the whole
Of life in a new rhythm. The cup of dole
God gave for baptism, I am fain to drink,
And praise its sweetness, Sweet, with thee anear.
The names of country, heaven, are changed away
For where thou art or shalt be, there or here;
And this . . . this lute and song . . . loved yesterday,
(The singing angels know) are only dear
Because thy name moves right in what they say.

VIII

WHAT can I give thee back, O liberal
And princely giver, who hast brought the gold
And purple of thine heart, unstained, untold,
And laid them on the outside of the wall
For such as I to take or leave withal,
In unexpected largesse? am I cold,
Ungrateful, that for these most manifold
High gifts, I render nothing back at all?
Not so; not cold,—but very poor instead.
Ask God who knows. For frequent tears have run
The colours from my life, and left so dead
And pale a stuff, it were not fitly done
To give the same as pillow to thy head.
Go farther! let it serve to trample on.

IX

CAN it be right to give what I can give
To let thee sit beneath the fall of tears
As salt as mine, and hear the sighing years
Re-sighing on my lips renunciative
Through those infrequent smiles which fail to live
For all thy adjurations? O my fears,
That this can scarce be right! We are not peers,
So to be lovers; and I own, and grieve,
That givers of such gifts as mine are, must
Be counted with the ungenerous. Out, alas!
I will not soil thy purple with my dust,
Nor breathe my poison on thy Venice-glass,
Nor give thee any love—which were unjust.
Beloved, I only love thee! let it pass.

X

YET, love, mere love, is beautiful indeed
And worthy of acceptation. Fire is bright,
Let temple burn, or flax; an equal light
Leaps in the flame from cedar-plank or weed:
And love is fire. And when I say at need
I love thee . . . mark! . . . *I love thee*—in thy sight
I stand transfigured, glorified aright,
With conscience of the new rays that proceed
Out of my face toward thine. There's nothing low
In love, when love the lowest: meanest creatures
Who love God, God accepts while loving so.
And what I *feel*, across the inferior features
Of what I *am*, doth flash itself, and show
How that great work of Love enhances Nature's.

XI

AND therefore if to love can be desert,
I am not all unworthy. Cheeks as pale
As these you see, and trembling knees that fail
To bear the burden of a heavy heart,—
This weary minstrel-life that once was girt
To climb Aornus, and can scarce avail
To pipe now 'gainst the valley nightingale
A melancholy music,—why advert
To these things? O Belovèd, it is plain
I am not of thy worth nor for thy place!
And yet, because I love thee, I obtain
From that same love this vindicating grace,
To live on still in love, and yet in vain,—
To bless thee, yet renounce thee to thy face.

XII

INDEED this very love which is my boast,
And which, when rising up from breast to brow,
Doth crown me with a ruby large enow
To draw men's eyes and prove the inner cost,—
This love even, all my worth, to the uttermost,
I should not love withal, unless that thou
Hadst set me an example, shown me how,
When first thine earnest eyes with mine were crossed,
And love called love. And thus, I cannot speak
Of love even, as a good thing of my own:
Thy soul hath snatched up mine all faint and weak,
And placed it by thee on a golden throne,—
And that I love (O soul, we must be meek!)
Is by thee only, whom I love alone.

XIII

AND wilt thou have me fashion into speech
The love I bear thee, finding words enough,
And hold the torch out, while the winds are rough,
Between our faces, to cast light on each? —
I drop it at thy feet. I cannot teach
My hand to hold my spirit so far off
From myself—me—that I should bring thee proof
In words, of love hid in me out of reach.
Nay, let the silence of my womanhood
Commend my woman-love to thy belief,—
Seeing that I stand unwon, however wooed,
And rend the garment of my life, in brief,
By a most dauntless, voiceless fortitude,
Lest one touch of this heart convey its grief.

XIV

IF thou must love me, let it be for nought
Except for love's sake only. Do not say
"I love her for her smile—her look—her way
Of speaking gently,—for a trick of thought
That falls in well with mine, and certes brought
A sense of pleasant ease on such a day"—
For these things in themselves, Belovèd, may
Be changed, or change for thee,—and love, so wrought,
May be unwrought so. Neither love me for
Thine own dear pity's wiping my cheeks dry,—
A creature might forget to weep, who bore
Thy comfort long, and lose thy love thereby!
But love me for love's sake, that evermore
Thou mayst love on, through love's eternity.

XV

ACCUSE me not, beseech thee, that I wear
Too calm and sad a face in front of thine;
For we two look two ways, and cannot shine
With the same sunlight on our brow and hair.
On me thou lookest with no doubting care,
As on a bee shut in a crystalline;
Since sorrow hath shut me safe in love's divine,
And to spread wing and fly in the outer air
Were most impossible failure, if I strove
To fail so. But I look on thee—on thee—
Beholding, besides love, the end of love,
Hearing oblivion beyond memory;
As one who sits and gazes from above,
Over the rivers to the bitter sea.

XVI

AND yet, because thou overcomest so,
Because thou art more noble and like a king,
Thou canst prevail against my fears and fling
Thy purple round me, till my heart shall grow
Too close against thine heart henceforth to know
How it shook when alone. Why, conquering
May prove as lordly and complete a thing
In lifting upward, as in crushing low!
And as a vanquished soldier yields his sword
To one who lifts him from the bloody earth,
Even so, Belovèd, I at last record,
Here ends my strife. If *thou* invite me forth,
I rise above abasement at the word.
Make thy love larger to enlarge my worth.

XVII

MY poet, thou canst touch on all the notes
God set between His After and Before,
And strike up and strike off the general roar
Of the rushing worlds a melody that floats
In a serene air purely. Antidotes
Of medicated music, answering for
Mankind's forlornest uses, thou canst pour
From thence into their ears. God's will devotes
Thine to such ends, and mine to wait on thine.
How, Dearest, wilt thou have me for most use?
A hope, to sing by gladly? of a fine
Sad memory, with thy songs to interfuse?
A shade, in which to sing—of palm or pine?
A grave, on which to rest from singing? Choose.

XVIII

I NEVER gave a lock of hair away
To a man, Dearest, except this to thee,
Which now upon my fingers thoughtfully,
I ring out to the full brown length and say
"Take it." My day of youth went yesterday;
My hair no longer bounds to my foot's glee,
Nor plant I it from rose or myrtle-tree,
As girls do, any more: it only may
Now shade on two pale cheeks the mark of tears,
Taught drooping from the head that hangs aside
Through sorrow's trick. I thought the funeral-shears
Would take this first, but Love is justified,—
Take it thou,—finding pure, from all those years,
The kiss my mother left here when she died.

XIX

THE soul's Rialto hath its merchandise;
I barter curl for curl upon that mart,
And from my poet's forehead to my heart
Receive this lock which outweighs argosies,
As purply black, as erst to Pindar's eyes
The dim purpureal tresses gloomed athwart
The nine white Muse-brows. For this counterpart,
The bay-crown's shade, Belovèd, I surmise,
Still lingers on thy curl, it is so black!
Thus, with a fillet of smooth-kissing breath,
I tie the shadows safe from gliding back,
And lay the gift where nothing hindereth;
Here on my heart, as on thy brow, to lack
No natural heat till mine grows cold in death.

XX

BELOVED, my Belovèd, when I think
That thou wast in the world a year ago,
What time I sat alone here in the snow
And saw no footprint, heard the silence sink
No moment at thy voice, but, link by link,
Went counting all my chains as if that so
They never could fall off at any blow
Struck by thy possible hand,—why, thus I drink
Of life's great cup of wonder! Wonderful,
Never to feel thee thrill the day or night
With personal act or speech,—nor ever cull
Some prescience of thee with the blossoms white
Thou sawest growing! Atheists are as dull,
Who cannot guess God's presence out of sight.

XXI

SAY over again, and yet once over again,
That thou dost love me. Though the word repeated
Should seem "a cuckoo-song," as thou dost treat it,
Remember, never to the hill or plain,
Valley and wood, without her cuckoo-strain
Comes the fresh Spring in all her green completed.
Belovèd, I, amid the darkness greeted
By a doubtful spirit-voice, in that doubt's pain
Cry, "Speak once more—thou lovest!" Who can fear
Too many stars, though each in heaven shall roll,
Too many flowers, though each shall crown the year?
Say thou dost love me, love me, love me—toll
The silver iterance!—only minding, Dear,
To love me also in silence with thy soul.

XXII

WHEN our two souls stand up erect and strong,
Face to face, silent, drawing nigh and nigher,
Until the lengthening wings break into fire
At either curved point,—what bitter wrong
Can the earth do to us, that we should not long
Be here contented? Think. In mounting higher,
The angels would press on us and aspire
To drop some golden orb of perfect song
Into our deep, dear silence. Let us stay
Rather on earth, Belovèd,—where the unfit
Contrarious moods of men recoil away
And isolate pure spirits, and permit
A place to stand and love in for a day,
With darkness and the death-hour rounding it.

XXIII

IS it indeed so? If I lay here dead,
Wouldst thou miss any life in losing mine?
And would the sun for thee more coldly shine
Because of grave-damps falling round my head?
I marvelled, my Belovèd, when I read
Thy thought so in the letter. I am thine—
But . . . *so* much to thee? Can I pour thy wine
While my hands tremble? Then my soul, instead
Of dreams of death, resumes life's lower range.
Then, love me, Love! look on me—breathe on me!
As brighter ladies do not count it strange,
For love, to give up acres and degree,
I yield the grave for thy sake, and exchange
My near sweet view of Heaven, for earth with thee!

XXIV

LET the world's sharpness, like a clasping knife,
Shut in upon itself and do no harm
In this close hand of Love, now soft and warm,
And let us hear no sound of human strife
After the click of the shutting. Life to life—
I lean upon thee, Dear, without alarm,
And feel as safe as guarded by a charm
Against the stab of worldlings, who if rife
Are weak to injure. Very whitely still
The lilies of our lives may reassure
Their blossoms from their roots, accessible
Alone to heavenly dews that drop not fewer,
Growing straight, out of man's reach, on the hill.
God only, who made us rich, can make us poor.

XXV

A HEAVY heart, Belovèd, have I borne
From year to year until I saw thy face,
And sorrow after sorrow took the place
Of all those natural joys as lightly worn
As the stringed pearls, each lifted in its turn
By a beating heart at dance-time. Hopes apace
Were changed to long despairs, till God's own grace
Could scarcely lift above the world forlorn
My heavy heart. Then *thou* didst bid me bring
And let it drop adown thy calmly great
Deep being! Fast it sinketh, as a thing
Which its own nature doth precipitate,
While thine doth close above it, mediating
Betwixt the stars and the unaccomplished fate.

XXVI

I LIVED with visions for my company
Instead of men and women, years ago,
And found them gentle mates, nor thought to know
A sweeter music than they played to me.
But soon their trailing purple was not free
Of this world's dust, their lutes did silent grow,
And I myself grew faint and blind below
Their vanishing eyes. Then *thou* didst come—to be,
Belovèd, what they seemed. Their shining fronts,
Their songs, their splendours (better, yet the same,
As river-water hallowed into fonts),
Met in thee, and from out thee overcame
My soul with satisfaction of all wants:
Because God's gifts put man's best dreams to shame.

XXVII

MY own Belovèd, who hast lifted me
From this drear flat of earth where I was thrown,
And, in betwixt the languid ringlets, blown
A life-breath, till the forehead hopefully
Shines out again, as all the angels see,
Before thy saving kiss! My own, my own,
Who camest to me when the world was gone,
And I who looked for only God, found *thee*!
I find thee; I am safe, and strong, and glad.
As one who stands in dewless asphodel
Looks backward on the tedious time he had
In the upper life,—so I, with bosom-swell,
Make witness, here, between the good and bad,
That Love, as strong as Death, retrieves as well.

XXVIII

MY letters! all dead paper, mute and white!
And yet they seem alive and quivering
Against my tremulous hands which loose the string
And let them drop down on my knee to-night.
This said,—he wished to have me in his sight
Once, as a friend: this fixed a day in spring
To come and touch my hand . . . a simple thing,
Yet I wept for it!—this, . . . the paper's light . . .
Said, *Dear, I love thee;* and I sank and quailed
As if God's future thundered on my past.
This said, *I am thine*—and so its ink has paled
With lying at my heart that beat too fast.
And this . . . O Love, thy words have ill availed
If, what this said, I dared repeat at last!

XXIX

I THINK of thee!—my thoughts do twine and bud
About thee, as wild vines, about a tree,
Put out broad leaves, and soon there's nought to see
Except the straggling green which hides the wood.
Yet, O my palm-tree, be it understood
I will not have my thoughts instead of thee
Who art dearer, better! Rather, instantly
Renew thy presence; as a strong tree should,
Rustle thy boughs and set thy trunk all bare,
And let these bands of greenery which insphere thee
Drop heavily down,—burst, shattered, everywhere!
Because, in this deep joy to see and hear thee
And breathe within thy shadow a new air,
I do not think of thee—I am too near thee.

XXX

I SEE thine image through my tears to-night,
And yet to-day I saw thee smiling. How
Refer the cause?—Belovèd, is it thou
Or I, who makes me sad? The acolyte
Amid the chanted joy and thankful rite
May so fall flat, with pale insensate brow,
On the altar-stair. I hear thy voice and vow,
Perplexed, uncertain, since thou art out of sight,
As he, in his swooning ears, the choir's Amen.
Belovèd, dost thou love? or did I see all
The glory as I dreamed, and fainted when
Too vehement light dilated my ideal,
For my soul's eyes? Will that light come again,
As now these tears come—falling hot and real?

XXXI

THOU comest! all is said without a word.
I sit beneath thy looks, as children do
In the noon-sun, with souls that tremble through
Their happy eyelids from an unaverred
Yet prodigal inward joy. Behold, I erred
In that last doubt! and yet I cannot rue
The sin most, but the occasion—that we two
Should for a moment stand unministered
By a mutual presence. Ah, keep near and close,
Thou dovelike help! and, when my fears would rise,
With thy broad heart serenely interpose:
Brood down with thy divine sufficiencies
These thoughts which tremble when bereft of those,
Like callow birds left desert to the skies.

XXXII

THE first time that the sun rose on thine oath
To love me, I looked forward to the moon
To slacken all those bonds which seemed too soon
And quickly tied to make a lasting troth.
Quick-loving hearts, I thought, may quickly loathe;
And, looking on myself, I seemed not one
For such man's love!—more like an out-of-tune
Worn viol, a good singer would be wroth
To spoil his song with, and which, snatched in haste,
Is laid down at the first ill-sounding note.
I did not wrong myself so, but I placed
A wrong on *thee*. For perfect strains may float
'Neath master-hands, from instruments defaced,—
And great souls, at one stroke, may do and doat.

XXXIII

YES, call me by my pet-name! let me hear
The name I used to run at, when a child,
From innocent play, and leave the cowslips piled,
To glance up in some face that proved me dear
With the look of its eyes. I miss the clear
Fond voices which, being drawn and reconciled
Into the music of Heaven's undefiled,
Call me no longer. Silence on the bier,
While I call God—call God!—So let thy mouth
Be heir to those who are now exanimate.
Gather the north flowers to complete the south,
And catch the early love up in the late.
Yes, call me by that name,—and I, in truth,
With the same heart, will answer and not wait.

XXXIV

WITH the same heart, I said, I'll answer thee
As those, when thou shalt call me by my name—
Lo, the vain promise! is the same, the same,
Perplexed and ruffled by life's strategy?
When called before, I told how hastily
I dropped my flowers or brake off from a game,
To run and answer with the smile that came
At play last moment, and went on with me
Through my obedience. When I answer now,
I drop a grave thought, break from solitude;
Yet still my heart goes to thee—ponder how—
Not as to a single good, but all my good!
Lay thy hand on it, best one, and allow
That no child's foot could run fast as this blood.

XXXV

IF I leave all for thee, wilt thou exchange
And be all to me? Shall I never miss
Home-talk and blessing and the common kiss
That comes to each in turn, nor count it strange,
When I look up, to drop on a new range
Of walls and floors, another home than this?
Nay, wilt thou fill that place by me which is
Filled by dead eyes too tender to know change?
That's hardest. If to conquer love, has tried,
To conquer grief, tries more, as all things prove;
For grief indeed is love and grief beside.
Alas, I have grieved so I am hard to love.
Yet love me—wilt thou? Open thine heart wide,
And fold within the wet wings of thy dove.

XXXVI

WHEN we met first and loved, I did not build
Upon the event with marble. Could it mean
To last, a love set pendulous between
Sorrow and sorrow? Nay, I rather thrilled,
Distrusting every light that seemed to gild
The onward path, and feared to overlean
A finger even. And, though I have grown serene
And strong since then, I think that God has willed
A still renewable fear . . . O love, O troth . . .
Lest these enclaspèd hands should never hold,
This mutual kiss drop down between us both
As an unowned thing, once the lips being cold.
And Love, be false! if *he*, to keep one oath,
Must lose one joy, by his life's star foretold.

XXXVII

PARDON, oh, pardon, that my soul should make,
Of all that strong divineness which I know
For thine and thee, an image only so
Formed of the sand, and fit to shift and break.
It is that distant years which did not take
Thy sovranty, recoiling with a blow,
Have forced my swimming brain to undergo
Their doubt and dread, and blindly to forsake
Thy purity of likeness and distort
Thy worthiest love to a worthless counterfeit:
As if a shipwrecked Pagan, safe in port,
His guardian sea-god to commemorate,
Should set a sculptured porpoise, gills a-snort
And vibrant tail, within the temple-gate.

XXXVIII

FIRST time he kissed me, he but only kissed
The fingers of this hand wherewith I write;
And ever since, it grew more clean and white,
Slow to world-greetings, quick with its "Oh, list,"
When the angels speak. A ring of amethyst
I could not wear here, plainer to my sight,
Than that first kiss. The second passed in height
The first, and sought the forehead, and half missed,
Half falling on the hair. O beyond meed!
That was the chrism of love, which love's own crown,
With sanctifying sweetness, did precede.
The third upon my lips was folded down
In perfect, purple state; since when, indeed,
I have been proud and said, "My love, my own."

XXXIX

BECAUSE thou hast the power and own'st the grace
To look through and behind this mask of me
(Against which years have beat thus blanchingly
With their rains), and behold my soul's true face,
The dim and weary witness of life's race,—
Because thou hast the faith and love to see,
Through that same soul's distracting lethargy,
The patient angel waiting for a place
In the new Heavens,—because nor sin nor woe,
Nor God's infliction, nor death's neighbourhood,
Nor all which others viewing, turn to go,
Nor all which makes me tired of all, self-viewed,—
Nothing repels thee, . . . Dearest, teach me so
To pour out gratitude, as thou dost, good!

XL

OH, yes! they love through all this world of ours!
I will not gainsay love, called love forsooth.
I have heard love talked in my early youth,
And since, not so long back but that the flowers
Then gathered, smell still. Mussulmans and Giaours
Throw kerchiefs at a smile, and have no ruth
For any weeping. Polypheme's white tooth
Slips on the nut if, after frequent showers,
The shell is over-smooth,—and not so much
Will turn the thing called love, aside to hate
Or else to oblivion. But thou art not such
A lover, my Belovèd! thou canst wait
Through sorrow and sickness, to bring souls to touch,
And think it soon when others cry "Too late."

XLI

I THANK all who have loved me in their hearts,
With thanks and love from mine. Deep thanks to all
Who paused a little near the prison-wall
To hear my music in its louder parts
Ere they went onward, each one to the mart's
Or temple's occupation, beyond call.
But thou, who, in my voice's sink and fall
When the sob took it, thy divinest Art's
Own instrument didst drop down at thy foot
To hearken what I said between my tears, . . .
Instruct me how to thank thee! Oh, to shoot
My soul's full meaning into future years,
That *they* should lend it utterance, and salute
Love that endures, from Life that disappears!

XLII

"*My future will not copy fair my past*" —
I wrote that once; and thinking at my side
My ministering life-angel justified
The word by his appealing look upcast
To the white throne of God, I turned at last,
And there, instead, saw thee, not unallied
To angels in thy soul! Then I, long tried
By natural ills, received the comfort fast,
While budding, at thy sight, my pilgrim's staff
Gave out green leaves with morning dews impearled.
I seek no copy now of life's first half:
Leave here the pages with long musing curled,
And write me new my future's epigraph,
New angel mine, unhoped for in the world!

XLIII

HOW do I love thee? Let me count the ways.
I love thee to the depth and breadth and height
My soul can reach, when feeling out of sight
For the ends of Being and ideal Grace.
I love thee to the level of everyday's
Most quiet need, by sun and candle-light.
I love thee freely, as men strive for Right;
I love thee purely, as they turn from Praise.
I love thee with the passion put to use
In my old griefs, and with my childhood's faith.
I love thee with a love I seemed to lose
With my lost saints,—I love thee with the breath,
Smiles, tears, of all my life!—and, if God choose,
I shall but love thee better after death.

XLIV

BELOVED, thou hast brought me many flowers
Plucked in the garden, all the summer through
And winter, and it seemed as if they grew
In this close room, nor missed the sun and showers.
So, in the like name of that love of ours,
Take back these thoughts which here unfolded too,
And which on warm and cold days I withdrew
From my heart's ground. Indeed, those beds and bowers
Be overgrown with bitter weeds and rue,
And wait thy weeding; yet here's eglantine,
Here's ivy!—take them, as I used to do
Thy flowers, and keep them where they shall not pine.
Instruct thine eyes to keep their colours true,
And tell thy soul their roots are left in mine.

Epilogue

A REED

I AM no trumpet, but a reed:
No flattering breath shall from me lead
  A silver sound, a hollow sound!
I will not ring, for priest or king,
One blast that in re-echoing
  Would leave a bondsman faster bound.

I am no trumpet, but a reed:
Go, tell the fishers, as they spread
  Their nets along the river's edge,
I will not tear their nets at all,
Nor pierce their hands if they should fall:
  Then let them leave me in the sedge.

I am no trumpet, but a reed,—
A broken reed, the wind indeed
  Left flat upon a dismal shore:
Yet if a little maid, or child,
Should sigh within it, earnest-mild,
  This reed will answer evermore.

Robert Browning

Evelyn Hope

BEAUTIFUL Evelyn Hope is dead!
  Sit and watch by her side an hour.
That is her book-shelf, this her bed;
  She plucked that piece of geranium-flower,
Beginning to die too, in the glass;
  Little has yet been changed, I think:
The shutters are shut, no light may pass
  Save two long rays through the hinge's chink.

Sixteen years old when she died!
  Perhaps she had scarcely heard my name;
It was not her time to love; beside,
  Her life had many a hope and aim,
Duties enough and little cares,
  And now was quiet, now astir,
Till God's hand beckoned unawares,—
  And the sweet white brow is all of her.

Is it too late then, Evelyn Hope?
  What, your soul was pure and true,
The good stars met in your horoscope,
  Made you of spirit, fire and dew—
And, just because I was thrice as old
  And our paths in the world diverged so wide,
Each was nought to each, must I be told?
  We were fellow mortals, nought beside?

No, indeed! for God above
  Is great to grant, as mighty to make,

And creates the love to reward the love,
  I claim you still, for my own love's sake!
Delayed it may be for more lives yet,
  Through worlds I shall traverse, not a few:
Much is to learn, much to forget
  Ere the time be come for taking you.

But the time will come, — at last it will,
  When, Evelyn Hope, what meant (I shall say)
In the lower earth, in the years long still,
  That body and soul so pure and gay?
Why your hair was amber, I shall divine,
  And your mouth of your own geranium's red —
And what you would do with me, in fine,
  In the new life come in the old one's stead.

I have lived (I shall say) so much since then,
  Given up myself so many times,
Gained me the gains of various men,
  Ransacked the ages, spoiled the climes;
Yet one thing, one, in my soul's full scope,
  Either I missed or itself missed me:
And I want and find you, Evelyn Hope!
  What is the issue? let us see!

I loved you, Evelyn, all the while.
  My heart seemed full as it could hold?
There was place and to spare for the frank young smile,
  And the red young mouth, and the hair's young gold.
So, hush, — I will give you this leaf to keep:
  See, I shut it inside the sweet cold hand!
There, that is our secret: go to sleep!
  You will wake, and remember, and understand.

Love among the Ruins

I

WHERE the quiet-coloured end of evening smiles,
Miles and miles
On the solitary pastures where our sheep
Half-asleep
Tinkle homeward thro' the twilight, stray or stop
As they crop—
Was the site once of a city great and gay,
(So they say)
Of our country's very capital, its prince
Ages since
Held his court in, gathered councils, wielding far
Peace or war.

II

Now,—the country does not even boast a tree,
As you see,
To distinguish slopes of verdure, certain rills
From the hills
Intersect and give a name to, (else they run
Into one)
Where the domed and daring palace shot its spires
Up like fires
O'er the hundred-gated circuit of a wall
Bounding all,
Made of marble, men might march on nor be pressed,
Twelve abreast.

III

And such plenty and perfection, see, of grass
Never was!

Such a carpet as, this summer-time, o'erspreads
            And embeds
Every vestige of the city, guessed alone,
            Stock or stone—
Where a multitude of men breathed joy and woe
            Long ago;
Lust of glory pricked their hearts up, dread of shame
            Struck them tame;
And that glory and that shame alike, the gold
            Bought and sold.

IV

Now,—the single little turret that remains
            On the plains,
By the caper overrooted, by the gourd
            Overscored,
While the patching houseleek's head of blossom winks
            Through the chinks—
Marks the basement whence a tower in ancient time
            Sprang sublime,
And a burning ring, all round, the chariots traced
            As they raced,
And the monarch and his minions and his dames
            Viewed the games.

V

And I know, while thus the quiet-coloured eve
            Smiles to leave
To their folding, all our many-tinkling fleece
            In such peace,
And the slopes and rills in undistinguished grey
            Melt away—

That a girl with eager eyes and yellow hair
    Waits me there
In the turret whence the charioteers caught soul
    For the goal,
When the king looked, where she looks now, breathless,
  dumb
    Till I come.

VI

But he looked upon the city, every side,
    Far and wide,
All the mountains topped with temples, all the glades'
    Colonnades,
All the causeys, bridges, aqueducts,—and then,
    All the men!
When I do come, she will speak not, she will stand,
    Either hand
On my shoulder, give her eyes the first embrace
    Of my face,
Ere we rush, ere we extinguish sight and speech
    Each on each.

VII

In one year they sent a million fighters forth
    South and North,
And they built their gods a brazen pillar high
    As the sky,
Yet reserved a thousand chariots in full force—
    Gold, of course.
Oh heart! oh blood that freezes, blood that burns!
    Earth's returns

For whole centuries of folly, noise and sin!
Shut them in,
With their triumphs and their glories and the rest!
Love is best.

Song

I

NAY but you, who do not love her,
  Is she not pure gold, my mistress?
Holds earth aught—speak truth—above her?
  Aught like this tress, see, and this tress,
And this last fairest tress of all,
So fair, see, ere I let it fall?

II

Because, you spend your lives in praising;
  To praise, you search the wide world over:
Then why not witness, calmly gazing,
  If earth holds aught—speak truth—above her?
Above this tress, and this, I touch
But cannot praise, I love so much!

A Woman's Last Word

I

LET'S contend no more, Love,
  Strive nor weep:
All be as before, Love,
  —Only sleep!

II

What so wild as words are?
  I and thou
In debate, as birds are,
  Hawk on bough!

III

See the creature stalking
  While we speak!
Hush and hide the talking,
  Cheek on cheek!

IV

What so false as truth is,
  False to thee?
Where the serpent's tooth is
  Shun the tree—

V

Where the apple reddens
  Never pry—
Lest we lose our Edens,
  Eve and I.

VI

Be a god and hold me
With a charm!
Be a man and fold me
With thine arm!

VII

Teach me, only teach, Love!
As I ought
I will speak thy speech, Love,
Think thy thought—

VIII

Meet, if thou require it,
Both demands,
Laying flesh and spirit
In thy hands.

IX

That shall be to-morrow
Not to-night:
I must bury sorrow
Out of sight:

X

—Must a little weep, Love,
(Foolish me!)
And so fall asleep, Love,
Loved by thee.

Songs from "Pippa Passes"

1

GIVE her but a least excuse to love me!
When—where—
How—can this arm establish her above me,
If fortune fixed her as my lady there,
There already, to eternally reprove me?
("Hist!"—said Kate the Queen;
But "Oh!" cried the maiden, binding her tresses,
" 'Tis only a page that carols unseen,
Crumbling your hounds their messes!")

Is she wronged?—To the rescue of her honor,
My heart!
Is she poor?—What costs it to be styled a donor?
Merely an earth to cleave, a sea to part.
But that fortune should have thrust all this upon her!
("Nay, list!"—bade Kate the Queen;
And still cried the maiden, binding her tresses,
" 'Tis only a page that carols unseen,
Fitting your hawks their jesses!")

2

You'll love me yet!—and I can tarry
  Your love's protracted growing:
June reared that bunch of flowers you carry,
  From seeds of April's sowing.

I plant a heartfull now: some seed
  At least is sure to strike,

And yield—what you'll not pluck indeed,
  Not love, but, may be, like.

You'll look at least on love's remains,
  A grave's one violet:
Your look?—that pays a thousand pains.
  What's death? You'll love me yet!

Earth's Immortalities

FAME

SEE, as the prettiest graves will do in time,
Our poet's wants the freshness of its prime;
Spite of the sexton's browsing horse, the sods
Have struggled through its binding osier rods;
Headstone and half-sunk footstone lean awry,
Wanting the brick-work promised by-and-by;
How the minute grey lichens, plate o'er plate,
Have softened down the crisp-cut name and date!

LOVE

So, the year's done with!
(Love me for ever!)
All March begun with,
April's endeavour;
May-wreaths that bound me
June needs must sever;
Now snows fall round me,
Quenching June's fever—
(Love me for ever!)

Meeting at Night

I

THE grey sea and the long black land;
And the yellow half-moon large and low;
And the startled little waves that leap
In fiery ringlets from their sleep,
As I gain the cove with pushing prow,
And quench its speed i' the slushy sand.

II

Then a mile of warm sea-scented beach;
Three fields to cross till a farm appears;
A tap at the pane, the quick sharp scratch
And blue spurt of a lighted match,
And a voice less loud, thro' its joys and fears,
Than the two hearts beating each to each!

Parting at Morning

ROUND the cape of a sudden came the sea,
And the sun looked over the mountain's rim:
And straight was a path of gold for him,
And the need of a world of men for me.

A Light Woman

SO far as our story approaches the end,
  Which do you pity the most of us three?—
My friend, or the mistress of my friend
  With her wanton eyes, or me?

My friend was already too good to lose,
  And seemed in the way of improvement yet,
When she crossed his path with her hunting-noose,
  And over him drew her net.

When I saw him tangled in her toils,
  A shame, said I, if she adds just him
To her nine-and-ninety other spoils,
  The hundredth for a whim!

And before my friend be wholly hers,
  How easy to prove to him, I said,
An eagle's the game her pride prefers,
  Though she snaps at a wren instead!

So, I gave her eyes my own eyes to take,
  My hand sought hers as in earnest need,
And round she turned for my noble sake,
  And gave me herself indeed.

The eagle am I, with my fame in the world,
  The wren is he, with his maiden face.
—You look away and your lip is curled?
  Patience, a moment's space!

For see, my friend goes shaking and white;
He eyes me as the basilisk:
I have turned, it appears, his day to night,
Eclipsing his sun's disk.

And I did it, he thinks, as a very thief:
"Though I love her—that, he comprehends—
One should master one's passions, (love, in chief)
And be loyal to one's friends!"

And she,—she lies in my hand as tame
As a pear late basking over a wall;
Just a touch to try and off it came;
'Tis mine,—can I let it fall?

With no mind to eat it, that's the worst!
Were it thrown in the road, would the case assist?
'Twas quenching a dozen blue-flies' thirst
When I gave its stalk a twist.

And I,—what I seem to my friend, you see:
What I soon shall seem to his love, you guess:
What I seem to myself, do you ask of me?
No hero, I confess.

'Tis an awkward thing to play with souls,
And matter enough to save one's own:
Yet think of my friend, and the burning coals
He played with for bits of stone!

One likes to show the truth for the truth;
  That the woman was light is very true:
But suppose she says,—Never mind that youth!
  What wrong have I done to you?

Well, anyhow, here the story stays,
  So far at least as I understand;
And, Robert Browning, you writer of plays,
  Here's a subject made to your hand!

The Last Ride Together

I SAID—Then, dearest, since 'tis so,
Since now at length my fate I know,
Since nothing all my love avails,
Since all, my life seemed meant for, fails,
   Since this was written and needs must be—
My whole heart rises up to bless
Your name in pride and thankfulness!
Take back the hope you gave,—I claim
Only a memory of the same,
—And this beside, if you will not blame,
   Your leave for one more last ride with me.

My mistress bent that brow of hers;
Those deep dark eyes where pride demurs
When pity would be softening through,
Fixed me a breathing-while or two
   With life or death in the balance: right!
The blood replenished me again;
My last thought was at least not vain:
I and my mistress, side by side
Shall be together, breathe and ride,
So, one day more am I deified.
   Who knows but the world may end to-night?

Hush! if you saw some western cloud
All billowy-bosomed, over-bowed
By many benedictions—sun's
And moon's and evening-star's at once—
   And so, you, looking and loving best,

Conscious grew, your passion drew
Cloud, sunset, moonrise, star-shine too,
Down on you, near and yet more near,
Till flesh must fade for heaven was here!—
Thus leant she and lingered—joy and fear!
   Thus lay she a moment on my breast.

Then we began to ride. My soul
Smoothed itself out, a long-cramped scroll
Freshening and fluttering in the wind.
Past hopes already lay behind.
   What need to strive with a life awry?
Had I said that, had I done this,
So might I gain, so might I miss.
Might she have loved me? just as well
She might have hated, who can tell!
Where had I been now if the worst befell
   And here we are riding, she and I.

Fail I alone, in words and deeds?
Why, all men strive, and who succeeds?
We rode; it seemed my spirit flew,
Saw other regions, cities new,
   As the world rushed by on either side.
I thought,—All labor, yet no less
Bear up beneath their unsuccess.
Look at the end of work, contrast
The petty done, the undone vast,
This present of theirs with the hopeful past!
   I hoped she would love me; here we ride.

What hand and brain went ever paired?
What heart alike conceived and dared?
What act proved all its thought had been?
What will but felt the fleshly screen?
  We ride and I see her bosom heave.
There's many a crown for who can reach.
Ten lines, a statesman's life in each!
The flag stuck on a heap of bones,
A soldier's doing! what atones?
They scratch his name on the Abbey-stones.
  My riding is better, by their leave.

What does it all mean, poet? Well,
Your brains beat into rhythm, you tell
What we felt only; you expressed
You hold things beautiful the best,
  And place them in rhyme so, side by side.
'Tis something, nay 'tis much: but then,
Have you yourself what's best for men?
Are you—poor, sick, old ere your time—
Nearer one whit your own sublime
Than we who never have turned a rhyme?
  Sing, riding's a joy! For me, I ride.

And you, great sculptor—so, you gave
A score of years to Art, her slave,
And that's your Venus, whence we turn
To yonder girl that fords the burn!
  You acquiesce, and shall I repine?
What, man of music, you grown grey
With notes and nothing else to say,
Is this your sole praise from a friend,

"Greatly his opera's strains intend,
But in music we know how fashions end!"
  I gave my youth; but we ride, in fine.

Who knows what's fit for us? Had fate
Proposed bliss here should sublimate
My being—had I signed the bond—
Still one must lead some life beyond,
  Have a bliss to die with, dim-described.
This foot once planted on the goal,
This glory-garland round my soul,
Could I descry such? Try and test!
I sink back shuddering from the quest.
Earth being so good, would heaven seem best?
  Now, heaven and she are beyond this ride.

And yet—she has not spoke so long!
What if heaven be that, fair and strong
At life's best, with our eyes upturned
Whither life's flower is first discerned,
  We, fixed so, ever should so abide?
What if we still ride on, we two,
With life forever old yet new,
Changed not in kind but in degree,
The instant made eternity,—
And heaven just prove that I and she
  Ride, ride together, forever ride?

Cristina

I

SHE should never have looked at me
  If she meant I should not love her!
There are plenty . . . men, you call such,
  I suppose . . . she may discover
All her soul to, if she pleases,
  And yet leave much as she found them:
But I'm not so, and she knew it
  When she fixed me, glancing round them.

II

What? To fix me thus meant nothing?
  But I can't tell (there's my weakness)
What her look said!—no vile cant, sure,
  About "need to strew the bleakness
Of some lone shore with its pearl seed.
  That the sea feels"—no "strange yearning
That such souls have, most to lavish
  Where there's chance of least returning."

III

Oh, we're sunk enough here, God knows!
  But not quite so sunk that moments,
Sure tho' seldom, are denied us,
  When the spirit's true endowments
Stand out plainly from its false ones,
  And apprise it if pursuing
Or the right way or the wrong way,
  To its triumph or undoing.

IV

There are flashes struck from midnights,
There are fire-flames noondays kindle,
Whereby piled-up honours perish,
Whereby swollen ambitions dwindle,
While just this or that poor impulse,
Which for once had play unstifled,
Seems the sole work of a life-time
That away the rest have trifled.

V

Doubt you if, in some such moment,
As she fixed me, she felt clearly,
Ages past the soul existed,
Here an age 'tis resting merely,
And hence fleets again for ages,
While the true end, sole and single,
It stops here for is, this love-way,
With some other soul to mingle?

VI

Else it loses what it lived for,
And eternally must lose it;
Better ends may be in prospect,
Deeper blisses (if you choose it),
But this life's end and this love-bliss
Have been lost here. Doubt you whether
This she felt as, looking at me,
Mine and her souls rushed together?

VII

Oh, observe! Of course, next moment,
The world's honours, in derision,

Trampled out the light for ever:
   Never fear but there's provision
Of the devil's to quench knowledge
   Lest we walk the earth in rapture!
—Making those who catch God's secret
   Just so much more prize their capture!

VIII

Such am I: the secret's mine now!
   She has lost me, I have gained her;
Her soul's mine: and thus, grown perfect,
   I shall pass my life's remainder.
Life will just hold out the proving
   Both our powers, alone and blended:
And then, come next life quickly!
   This world's use will have been ended.

The Lost Mistress

I

ALL'S over, then: does truth sound bitter
  As one at first believes?
Hark, 'tis the sparrows' good-night twitter
  About your cottage eaves!

II

And the leaf-buds on the vine are woolly,
  I noticed that, to-day;
One day more bursts them open fully
  —You know the red turns grey.

III

To-morrow we meet the same then, dearest?
  May I take your hand in mine?
Mere friends are we,—well, friends the merest
  Keep much that I resign:

IV

For each glance of the eye so bright and black,
  Though I keep with heart's endeavour,—
Your voice, when you wish the snowdrops back,
  Though it stay in my soul for ever!—

V

Yet I will but say what mere friends say,
  Or only a thought stronger;
I will hold your hand but as long as all may,
  Or so very little longer!

Home-Thoughts, From Abroad

I

OH, to be in England
Now that April's there,
And whoever wakes in England
Sees, some morning, unaware,
That the lowest boughs and the brushwood sheaf
Round the elm-tree bole are in tiny leaf,
While the chaffinch sings on the orchard bough
In England—now!

II

And after April, when May follows,
And the whitethroat builds, and all the swallows!
Hark, where my blossomed pear-tree in the hedge
Leans to the field and scatters on the clover
Blossoms and dewdrops—at the bent spray's edge—
That's the wise thrush; he sings each song twice over,
Lest you should think he never could recapture
The first fine careless rapture!
And though the fields look rough with hoary dew,
All will be gay when noontide wakes anew
The buttercups, the little children's dower
—Far brighter than this gaudy melon-flower!

Sonnet

EYES, calm beside thee (Lady, couldst thou know!)
May turn away thick with fast gathering tears:
I glance not where all gaze: thrilling and low
Their passionate praises reach thee—my cheek wears
Alone no wonder when thou passest by;
Thy tremulous lids, bent and suffused, reply
To the irrepressible homage which doth glow
On every lip but mine: if in thine ears
Their accents linger—and thou dost recall
Me as I stood, still, guarded, very pale,
Beside each votarist whose lighted brow
Wore worship like an aureole, "O'er them all
My beauty," thou wilt murmur, "did prevail
Save that one only:"—Lady, couldst thou know!

My Star

ALL that I know
  Of a certain star
Is, it can throw
  (Like the angled spar)
Now a dart of red,
  Now a dart of blue;
Till my friends have said
  They would fain see, too,
My star that dartles the red and the blue!
Then it stops like a bird; like a flower, hangs furled:
  They must solace themselves with the Saturn above it.
What matter to me if their star is a world?
  Mine has opened its soul to me; therefore I love it.

In a Gondola

HE SINGS

I SEND my heart up to thee, all my heart
  In this my singing.
For the stars help me, and the sea bears part;
  The very night is clinging
Closer to Venice' streets to leave one space
  Above me, whence thy face
May light my joyous heart to thee its dwelling-place.

SHE SPEAKS

Say after me, and try to say
My very words, as if each word
Came from you of your own accord,
In your own voice, in your own way:
"This woman's heart and soul and brain
Are mine as much as this gold chain
She bids me wear; which" (say again)
"I choose to make by cherishing
A precious thing, or choose to fling
Over the boat-side, ring by ring."
And yet once more say . . . no word more
Since words are only words. Give o'er!

Unless you call me, all the same,
Familiarly by my pet-name,
Which if the Three should hear you call,
And me reply to, would proclaim
At once our secret to them all.
Ask of me, too, command me, blame—

Do, break down the partition-wall
'Twixt us, the daylight world beholds
Curtained in dusk and splendid folds!
What's left but—all of me to take?
I am the Three's: prevent them, slake
Your thirst! 'Tis said, the Arab sage,
In practising with gems, can loose
Their subtle spirit in his cruce
And leave but ashes: so, sweet mage,
Leave them my ashes when thy use
Sucks out my soul, thy heritage!

HE SINGS

Past we glide, and past, and past!
  What's that poor Agnese doing
Where they make the shutters fast?
  Grey Zanobi's just a-wooing
To his couch the purchased bride:
  Past we glide!

Past we glide, and past, and past!
  Why's the Pucci Palace flaring
Like a beacon to the blast?
  Guests by hundreds, not one caring
If the dear host's neck were wried:
  Past we glide!

SHE SINGS

The moth's kiss, first!
Kiss me as if you made believe
You were not sure, this eve

How my face, your flower, had pursed
Its petals up; so, here and there
You brush it, till I grow aware
Who wants me, and wide ope I burst.

The bee's kiss, now!
Kiss me as if you entered gay
My heart at some noonday,
A bud that dares not disallow
The claim, so all is rendered up,
And passively its shattered cup
Over your head to sleep I bow.

HE SINGS

What are we two?
I am a Jew,
And carry thee, farther than friends can pursue,
To a feast of our tribe;
Where they need thee to bride
The devil that blasts them unless he imbide
Thy . . . Scatter the vision for ever! And now,
As of old, I am I, thou art thou!

Say again, what we are?
The sprite of a star,
I lure thee above where the destinies bar
My plumes their full play
Till a ruddier ray
Than my pale one announce there is withering away
Some . . . Scatter the vision for ever! And now,
As of old, I am I, thou art thou!

Oh, which were best, to roam or rest?
The land's lap or the water's breast?
To sleep on yellow millet-sheaves,
Or swim in lucid shallows just
Eluding water-lily leaves,
An inch from Death's black fingers, thrust
To lock you, whom release he must;
Which life were best on Summer eves?

HE SPEAKS, MUSING

Lie back; could thought of mine improve you?
From this shoulder let there spring
A wing; from this, another wing;
Wings, not legs and feet, shall move you!
Snow-white must they spring, to blend
With your flesh, but I intend
They shall deepen to the end,
Broader, into burning gold,
Till both wings crescent-wise enfold
Your perfect self, from 'neath your feet
To o'er your head, where, lo, they meet
As if a million sword-blades hurled
Defiance from you to the world!
Rescue me thou, the only real!
And scare away this mad ideal
That came, nor motions to depart!
Thanks! Now, stay ever as thou art!

STILL HE MUSES

What if the Three should catch at last
Thy serenader? While there's cast

Paul's cloak about my head, and fast
Gian pinions me, Himself has past
His stylet thro' my back; I reel;
And . . . is it thou I feel?

They trail me, these three godless knaves,
Past every church that saints and saves,
Nor stop till, where the cold sea raves
By Lido's wet accursed graves,
They scoop mine, roll me to its brink,
And . . . on thy breast I sink!

SHE REPLIES, MUSING

Dip your arm o'er the boat-side, elbow-deep,
As I do: thus: were death so unlike sleep,
Caught this way? Death's to fear from flame or steel,
Or poison doubtless; but from water—feel!
Go find the bottom! Would you stay me? There!
Now pluck a great blade of that ribbon-grass
To plait in where the foolish jewel was,
I flung away; since you have praised my hair,
'Tis proper to be choice in what I wear.

HE SPEAKS

Row home? must we row home? Too surely
Know I where its front's demurely
Over the Giudecca piled;
Window just with window mating,
Door on door exactly waiting,
All's the set face of a child:
But behind it, where's a trace

Of the staidness and reserve,
And formal lines without a curve,
In the same child's playing-face?
No two windows look one way
O'er the small sea-water thread
Below them. Ah, the autumn day
I, passing, saw you overhead!
First, out a cloud of curtain blew,
Then a sweet cry, and last came you—
To catch your lory [1] that must needs
Escape just then, of all times then,
To peck a tall plant's fleecy seeds,
And make me happiest of men.
I scarce could breathe to see you reach
So far back o'er the balcony
To catch him ere he climbed too high
Above you in the Smyrna peach
That quick the round smooth cord of gold,
This coiled hair on your head, unrolled,
Fell down you like a gorgeous snake
The Roman girls were wont, of old,
When Rome there was, for coolness' sake
To let lie curling o'er their bosoms.
Dear lory, may his beak retain
Ever its delicate rose stain
As if the wounded lotus-blossoms
Had marked their thief to know again!

Stay longer yet, for others' sake
Than mine! What should your chamber do?
—With all its rarities that ache
In silence while day lasts, but wake

[1] A parrot.

At night-time and their life renew,
Suspended just to pleasure you
Who brought against their will together
These objects, and, while day lasts, weave
Around them such a magic tether
That dumb they look; your harp, believe,
With all the sensitive tight strings
Which dare not speak, now to itself
Breathes slumberously, as if some elf
Went in and out the chords, his wings
Make murmur wheresoe'er they graze,
As an angel may, between the maze
Of midnight palace-pillars, on
And on, to sow God's plagues, have gone
Through guilty glorious Babylon.
And while such murmurs flow, the nymph
Bends o'er the harp-top from her shell
As the dry limpet for the lymph
Come with a tune he knows so well.
And how your statues' hearts must swell!
And how your pictures must descend
To see each other, friend with friend!
Oh, could you take them by surprise,
You'd find Schidone's eager Duke
Doing the quaintest courtesies
To that prim saint by Haste-thee-Luke!
And, deeper into her rock den,
Bold Castlefranco's Magdalen
You'd find retreated from the ken
Of that robed counsel-keeping Ser—
As if the Tizian thinks of her,
And is not, rather, gravely bent
On seeing for himself what toys

Are these, his progeny invent,
What litter now the board employs
Whereon he signed a document
That got him murdered! Each enjoys
Its night so well, you cannot break
The sport up, so, indeed must make
More stay with me, for others' sake.

SHE SPEAKS

To-morrow, if a harp-string, say,
Is used to tie the jasmine back
That overfloods my room with sweets,
Contrive your Zorzi somehow meets
My Zanze! If the ribbon's black,
The Three are watching: keep away!
Your gondola—let Zorzi wreathe
A mesh of water-weeds about
Its prow, as if he unaware
Had struck some quay or bridge-foot stair!
That I may throw a paper out
As you and he go underneath.

There's Zanze's vigilant tape; safe are we.
Only one minute more to-night with me?
Resume your past self of a month ago!
Be you the bashful gallant, I will be
The lady with the colder breast than snow.
Now bow you, as becomes, nor touch my hand
More than I touch yours when I step to land,
And say, "All thanks, Siora!"—
                                        Heart to heart
And lips to lips! Yet once more, ere we part,
Clasp me and make me thine, as mine thou art!

HE IS SURPRISED AND STABBED

It was ordained to be so, sweet! —and best
Comes now, beneath thine eyes, upon thy breast.
Still kiss me! Care not for the cowards! Care
Only to put aside thy beauteous hair
My blood will hurt! The Three, I do not scorn
To death, because they never lived: but I
Have lived indeed, and so— (yet one more kiss) —can die!

A Lovers' Quarrel

I

OH, what a dawn of day!
How the March sun feels like May!
  All is blue again
  After last night's rain,
And the South dries the hawthorn-spray.
  Only, my Love's away!
I'd as lief that the blue were grey.

II

Runnels, which rillets swell,
Must be dancing down the dell,
  With a foaming head
  On the beryl bed
Paven smooth as a hermit's cell;
  Each with a tale to tell,
Could my Love but attend as well.

III

Dearest, three months ago!
When we lived blocked-up with snow,—
  When the wind would edge
  In and in his wedge,
In, as far as the point could go—
  Not to our ingle, though,
Where we loved each the other so!

IV

Laughs with so little cause!
We devised games out of straws.

We would try and trace
One another's face
In the ash, as an artist draws;
Free on each other's flaws,
How we chattered like two church daws!

V

What's in the "Times"?—a scold
At the Emperor deep and cold;
He has taken a bride
To his gruesome side,
That's as fair as himself is bold:
There they sit ermine-stoled,
And she powders her hair with gold.

VI

Fancy the Pampas' sheen!
Miles and miles of gold and green
Where the sunflowers blow
In a solid glow,
And—to break now and then the screen—
Black neck and eyeballs keen,
Up a wild horse leaps between!

VII

Try, will our table turn?
Lay your hands there light, and yearn
Till the yearning slips
Thro' the finger-tips
In a fire which a few discern,
And a very few feel burn,
And the rest, they may live and learn!

VIII

Then we would up and pace,
For a change, about the place,
  Each with arm o'er neck:
  'Tis our quarter-deck,
We are seamen in woeful case.
  Help in the ocean-space!
Or, if no help, we'll embrace.

IX

See, how she looks now, dressed
In a sledging-cap and vest!
  'Tis a huge fur cloak—
  Like a reindeer's yoke
Falls the lappet along the breast:
  Sleeves for her arms to rest,
Or to hang, as my Love likes best.

X

Teach me to flirt a fan
As the Spanish ladies can,
  Or I tint your lip
  With a burnt stick's tip
And you turn into such a man!
  Just the two spots that span
Half the bill of the young male swan.

XI

Dearest, three months ago
When the mesmeriser Snow
  With his hand's first sweep
  Put the earth to sleep:

'Twas a time when the heart could show
  All—how was earth to know,
'Neath the mute hand's to-and-fro?

XII

Dearest, three months ago
When we loved each other so,
  Lived and loved the same
  Till an evening came
When a shaft from the devil's bow
  Pierced to our ingle-glow,
And the friends were friend and foe!

XIII

Not from the heart beneath—
'Twas a bubble born of breath,
  Neither sneer nor vaunt,
  Nor reproach nor taunt.
See a word, how it severeth!
  Oh, power of life and death
In the tongue, as the Preacher saith!

XIV

Woman, and will you cast
For a word, quite off at last
  Me, your own, your You,—
  Since, as truth is true,
I was You all the happy past—
  Me do you leave aghast
With the memories We amassed?

XV

Love, if you knew the light
That your soul casts in my sight,

How I look to you
For the pure and true
And the beauteous and the right,—
Bear with a moment's spite
When a mere mote threats the white!

XVI

What of a hasty word?
Is the fleshly heart not stirred
By a worm's pin-prick
Where its roots are quick?
See the eye, by a fly's foot blurred—
Ear, when a straw is heard
Scratch the brain's coat of curd!

XVII

Foul be the world or fair
More or less, how can I care?
'Tis the world the same
For my praise or blame,
And endurance is easy there.
Wrong in the one thing rare—
Oh, it is hard to bear!

XVIII

Here's the spring back or close,
When the almond-blossom blows:
We shall have the word
In a minor third
There is none but the cuckoo knows:
Heaps of the guelder-rose!
I must bear with it, I suppose.

XIX

Could but November come,
Were the noisy birds struck dumb
  At the warning slash
  Of his driver's-lash—
I would laugh like the valiant Thumb
  Facing the castle glum
And the giant's fee-faw-fum!

XX

Then, were the world well stripped
Of the gear wherein equipped
  We can stand apart,
  Heart dispense with heart
In the sun, with the flowers unnipped,—
  Oh, the world's hangings ripped,
We were both in a bare-walled crypt!

XXI

Each in the crypt would cry
"But one freezes here! and why?
  When a heart, as chill,
  At my own would thrill
Back to life, and its fires out-fly?
  Heart, shall we live or die?
The rest, . . . settle by-and-by!"

XXII

So, she'd efface the score,
And forgive me as before.

It is twelve o'clock:
I shall hear her knock
In the worst of a storm's uproar,
I shall pull her through the door,
I shall have her for evermore!

The Flower's Name

I

HERE'S the garden she walked across,
  Arm in my arm, such a short while since:
Hark, now I push its wicket, the moss
  Hinders the hinges and makes them wince!
She must have reached this shrub ere she turned,
  As back with that murmur the wicket swung;
For she laid the poor snail, my chance foot spurned,
  To feed and forget it the leaves among.

II

Down this side of the gravel-walk
  She went while her robe's edge brushed the box:
And here she paused in her gracious talk
  To point me a moth on the milk-white phlox.
Roses, ranged in valiant row,
  I will never think that she passed you by!
She loves you noble roses, I know;
  But yonder, see, where the rock-plants lie!

III

This flower she stopped at, finger on lip,
  Stooped over, in doubt, as settling its claim;
Till she gave me, with pride to make no slip,
  Its soft meandering Spanish name.
What a name! Was it love or praise?
  Speech half-asleep or song half-awake?
I must learn Spanish, one of these days,
  Only for that slow sweet name's sake.

IV

Roses, if I live and do well,
  I may bring her, one of these days,
To fix you fast with as fine a spell,
  Fit you each with his Spanish phrase;
But do not detain me now; for she lingers
  There, like sunshine over the ground,
And ever I see her soft white fingers
  Searching after the bud she found.

V

Flower, you Spaniard, look that you grow not,
  Stay as you are and be loved for ever!
Bud, if I kiss you 'tis that you blow not:
  Mind, the shut pink mouth opens never!
For while it pouts, her fingers wrestle,
  Twinkling the audacious leaves between,
Till round they turn and down they nestle—
  Is not the dear mark still to be seen?

VI

Where I find her not, beauties vanish;
  Whither I follow her, beauties flee;
Is there no method to tell her in Spanish
  June's twice June since she breathed it with me?
Come, bud, show me the least of her traces,
  Treasure my lady's lightest footfall!
—Ah, you may flout and turn up your faces—
  Roses, you are not so fair after all!

"De Gustibus—"

I

YOUR ghost will walk, you lover of trees,
(If our loves remain)
In an English lane,
By a cornfield-side a-flutter with poppies.
Hark, those two in the hazel coppice—
A boy and a girl, if the good fates please,
Making love, say,—
The happier they!
Draw yourself up from the light of the moon,
And let them pass, as they will too soon,
With the bean-flowers' boon,
And the blackbird's tune,
And May, and June!

II

What I love best in all the world
Is a castle, precipice-encurled,
In a gash of the wind-grieved Apennine
Or look for me, old fellow of mine,
(If I get my head from out the mouth
O' the grave, and loose my spirit's bands,
And come again to the land of lands)—
In a seaside house to the farther South,
Where the baked cicala dies of drouth,
And one sharp tree—'tis a cypress—stands,
By the many hundred years red-rusted,
Rough iron-spiked, ripe fruit-o'ercrusted,
My sentinel to guard the sands
To the water's edge. For, what expands
Before the house, but the great opaque

Blue breadth of sea without a break?
While, in the house, for ever crumbles
Some fragment of the frescoed walls,
From blisters where a scorpion sprawls.
A girl bare-footed brings, and tumbles
Down on the pavement, green-flesh melons,
And says there's news to-day—the king
Was shot at, touched in the liver-wing,
Goes with his Bourbon arm in a sling:
—She hopes they have not caught the felons.
Italy, my Italy!
Queen Mary's saying serves for me—
(When fortune's malice
Lost her—Calais)—
Open my heart and you will see
Graved inside of it, "Italy."
Such lovers old are I and she:
So it always was, so shall ever be!

The Glove

(PETER RONSARD *loquitur*)

"HEIGHO," yawned one day King Francis,
"Distance all value enhances!
When a man's busy, why, leisure
Strikes him as wonderful pleasure:
'Faith, and at leisure once is he?
Straightway he wants to be busy.
Here we've got peace; and aghast I'm
Caught thinking war the true pastime.
Is there a reason in metre?
Give us your speech, master Peter!"
I who, if mortal dare say so,
Ne'er am at loss with my Naso,
"Sire," I replied, "joys prove cloudlets:
Men are the merest Ixions"—
Here the King whistled aloud, "Let's
—Heigho—go look at our lions!"
Such are the sorrowful chances
If you talk fine to King Francis.

And so, to the courtyard proceeding
Our company, Francis was leading,
Increased by new followers tenfold
Before he arrived at the penfold;
Lords, ladies, like clouds which bedizen
At sunset the western horizon.
And Sir De Lorge pressed 'mid the foremost
With the dame he professed to adore most.
Oh, what a face! One by fits eyed
Her, and the horrible pitside;

For the penfold surrounded a hollow
Which led where the eye scarce dared follow
And shelved to the chamber secluded
Where Bluebeard, the great lion, brooded.
The King hailed his keeper, an Arab
As glossy and black as a scarab,
And bade him make sport and at once stir
Up and out of his den the old monster.
They opened a hole in the wire-work
Across it, and dropped there a firework,
And fled: one's heart's beating redoubled:
A pause, while the pit's mouth was troubled.
The blackness and silence so utter,
By the firework's slow sparkling and sputter;
Then earth in a sudden contortion
Gave out to our gaze her abortion.
Such a brute! Were I friend Clement Marot
(Whose experience of nature's but narrow,
And whose faculties move in no small mist
When he versifies David the Psalmist)
I should study that brute to describe you
Illum Juda Leonem de Tribu.

One's whole blood grew curdling and creepy
To see the black mane, vast and heapy,
The tail in the air stiff and straining,
The wide eyes, nor waxing nor waning,
As over the barrier which bounded
His platform, and us who surrounded
The barrier, they reached and they rested
On space that might stand him in best stead:
For who knew, he thought, what the amazement,
The eruption of clatter and blaze meant,

And if, in this minute of wonder,
No outlet, 'mid lightning and thunder,
Lay broad, and, his shackles all shivered,
The lion at last was delivered?
Ay, that was the open sky o'erhead!
And you saw by the flash on his forehead,
By the hope in those eyes wide and steady,
He was leagues in the desert already,
Driving the flocks up the mountain,
Or catlike couched hard by the fountain
To waylay the date-gathering negress:
So guarded he entrance or egress.
"How he stands!" quoth the King: "we may well swear,
(No novice, we've won our spurs elsewhere
And so can afford the confession,)
We exercise wholesome discretion
In keeping aloof from his threshold,
Once hold you, those jaws want no fresh hold,
Their first would too pleasantly purloin
The visitor's brisket or surloin:
But who's he would prove so fool-hardy?
Not the best man of Marignan, pardie!"
The sentence no sooner was uttered,
Than over the rails a glove fluttered,
Fell close to the lion, and rested:
The dame 'twas, who flung it and jested
With life so, De Lorge had been wooing
For months past; he sat there pursuing
His suit, weighing out with nonchalance
Fine speeches like gold from a balance.

Sound the trumpet, no true knight's a tarrier!
De Lorge made one leap at the barrier,

Walked straight to the glove,—while the lion
Ne'er moved, kept his far-reaching eye on
The palm-tree-edged desert-spring's sapphire,
And the musky oiled skin of the Kaffir,—
Picked it up, and as calmly retreated,
Leaped back where the lady was seated,
And full in the face of its owner
Flung the glove.

"Your heart's queen, you dethrone her?
So should I!"—cried the King—" 'twas mere vanity,
Not love, set that task to humanity!"
Lords and ladies alike turned with loathing
From such a proved wolf in sheep's clothing.

Not so, I; for I caught an expression
In her brow's undisturbed self-possession
Amid the Court's scoffing and merriment,—
As if from no pleasing experiment
She rose, yet of pain not much heedful
So long as the process was needful,—
As if she had tried in a crucible,
To what "speeches like gold" were reducible.
And, finding the finest prove copper,
Felt the smoke in her face was but proper;
To know what she had *not* to trust to,
Was worth all the ashes and dust too.
She went out 'mid hooting and laughter;
Clement Marot stayed; I followed after,
And asked, as a grace, what it all meant?
If she wished not the rash deed's recallment?
"For I"—so I spoke—"am a poet:
Human nature,—behooves that I know it!"

She told me, "Too long had I heard
Of the deed proved alone by the word:
For my love—what De Lorge would not dare!
With my scorn—what De Lorge could compare!
And the endless descriptions of death
He would brave when my lip formed a breath,
I must reckon as braved, or, of course,
Doubt his word—and moreover, perforce,
For such gifts as no lady could spurn,
Must offer my love in return.
When I looked on your lion, it brought
All the dangers at once to my thought,
Encountered by all sorts of men,
Before he was lodged in his den,—
From the poor slave whose club or bare hands
Dug the trap, set the snare on the sands,
With no King and no Court to applaud,
By no shame, should he shrink, overawed,
Yet to capture the creature made shift,
That his rude boys might laugh at the gift,
—To the page who last leaped o'er the fence
Of the pit, on no greater pretence
Than to get back the bonnet he dropped,
Lest his pay for a week should be stopped.
So, wiser I judged it to make
One trial what 'death for my sake'
Really meant, while the power was yet mine,
Than to wait until time should define
Such a phrase not so simply as I,
Who took it to mean just 'to die.'
The blow a glove gives is but weak:
Does the mark yet discolor my cheek?

But when the heart suffers a blow,
Will the pain pass so soon, do you know?"

I looked, as away she was sweeping,
And saw a youth eagerly keeping
As close as he dared to the doorway.
No doubt that a noble should more weigh
His life than befits a plebeian;
And yet, had our brute been Nemean—
(I judge by a certain calm fervor
The youth stepped with, forward to serve her)
—He'd have scarce thought you did him the worst turn
If you whispered, "Friend, what you'd get, first earn!"
And when, shortly after, she carried
Her shame from the Court, and they married,
To that marriage some happiness, maugre
The voice of the Court, I dared augur.

For De Lorge, he made women with men vie,
Those in wonder and praise, these in envy;
And in short stood so plain a head taller
That he wooed and won . . . how do you call her?
The beauty, that rose in the sequel
To the King's love, who loved her a week well.
And 'twas noticed he never would honor
De Lorge (who looked daggers upon her)
With the easy commission of stretching
His legs in the service, and fetching
His wife, from her chamber, those straying
Sad gloves she was always mislaying,
While the King took the closet to chat in,—
But of course this adventure came pat in.

And never the King told the story,
How bringing a glove brought such glory,
But the wife smiled—"His nerves are grown firmer:
Mine he brings now and utters no murmur."

Venienti occurrite morbo!
With which moral I drop my theorbo.

By the Fireside

(The scene of the declaration in this poem is laid in a little mountain gorge adjacent to the Baths of Lucca, where the Brownings spent the summer of 1853.)

HOW well I know what I mean to do
  When the long dark autumn evenings come;
And where, my soul, is thy pleasant hue?
  With the music of all thy voices, dumb
In life's November too!

I shall be found by the fire, suppose,
  O'er a great wise book as beseemeth age,
While the shutters flap as the cross-wind blows,
  And I turn the page, and I turn the page,
Not verse now, only prose!

Till the young ones whisper, finger on lip,
  "There he is at it, deep in Greek:
Now then, or never, out we slip
  To cut from the hazels by the creek
A mainmast for our ship!"

I shall be at it indeed, my friends!
  Greek puts already on either side
Such a branch-work forth as soon extends
  To a vista opening far and wide,
And I pass out where it ends.

The outside-frame, like your hazel-trees—
  But the inside-archway widens fast,

And a rarer sort succeeds to these,
   And we slope to Italy at last
And youth, by green degrees.

I follow wherever I am led,
   Knowing so well the leader's hand:
Oh woman-country, wooed not wed,
   Loved all the more by earth's male-lands,
Laid to their hearts instead!

Look at the ruined chapel again
   Half-way up in the Alpine gorge!
Is that a tower, I point you plain,
   Or is it a mill, or an iron forge
Breaks solitude in vain?

A turn, and we stand in the heart of things;
   The woods are round us, heaped and dim;
From slab to slab how it slips and springs,
   The thread of water single and slim,
Through the ravage some torrent brings!

Does it feed the little lake below?
   That speck of white just on its marge
Is Pella; see, in the evening-glow,
   How sharp the silver spear-heads charge
When Alp meets heaven in snow!

On our other side is the straight-up rock;
   And a path is kept 'twixt the gorge and it

By boulder-stones where lichens mock
  The marks on a moth, and small ferns fit
Their teeth to the polished block.

Oh the sense of the yellow mountain-flowers,
  And thorny balls, each three in one,
The chestnuts throw on our path in showers!
  For the drop of the woodland fruit's begun
These early November hours,

That crimson the creeper's leaf across
  Like a splash of blood, intense, abrupt,
O'er a shield else gold from rim to boss,
  And lay it for show on the fairy-cupped
Elf-needled mat of moss,

By the rose-flesh mushrooms, undivulged
  Last evening—nay, in to-day's first dew
Yon sudden coral nipple bulged,
  Where a freaked fawn-colored flaky crew
Of toad-stools peep indulged.

And yonder, at foot of the fronting ridge
  That takes the turn to a range beyond,
Is the chapel reached by the one-arched bridge
  Where the water is stopped in a stagnant pond
Danced over by the midge.

The chapel and bridge are of stone alike,
  Blackish-grey and mostly wet;

Cut hemp-stalks steep in the narrow dyke.
See here again, how the lichens fret
And the roots of the ivy strike!

Poor little place, where its one priest comes
On a festa-day, if he comes at all,
To the dozen folk from their scattered homes,
Gathered within that precinct small
By the dozen ways one roams—

To drop from the charcoal-burners' huts,
Or climb from the hemp-dressers' low shed,
Leave the grange where the woodman stores his nuts,
Or the wattled cote where the fowlers spread
Their gear on the rock's bare juts.

It has some pretension too, this front,
With its bit of fresco half-moon-wise
Set over the porch, Art's early wont:
'Tis John in the Desert, I surmise,
But has borne the weather's brunt—

Not from the fault of the builder, though,
For a pent-house properly projects
Where three carved beams make a certain show,
Dating—good thought of our architect's—
'Five, six, nine, he lets you know.

And all day long a bird sings there,
And a stray sheep drinks at the pond at times;

The place is silent and aware;
  It has had its scenes, its joys and crimes,
But that is its own affair.

My perfect wife, my Leonor,
  Oh heart, my own, oh eyes, mine too,
Whom else could I dare look backward for,
  With whom beside should I dare pursue
The path grey heads abhor?

For it leads to a crag's sheer edge with them;
  Youth, flowery all the way, there stops—
Not they; age threatens and they contemn,
  Till they reach the gulf wherein youth drops,
One inch from life's safe hem!

With me, youth led . . . I will speak now,
  No longer watch you as you sit
Reading by fire-light, that great brow
  And the spirit-small hand propping it,
Mutely, my heart knows how—

When, if I think but deep enough,
  You are wont to answer, prompt as rhyme;
And you, too, find without rebuff
  Response your soul seeks many a time
Piercing its fine flesh-stuff.

My own, confirm me! If I tread
  This path back, is it not in pride

To think how little I dreamed it led
   To an age so blest that, by its side,
Youth seems the waste instead?

My own, see where the years conduct!
   At first, 'twas something our two souls
Should mix as mists do; each is sucked
   In each now: on, the new stream rolls,
Whatever rocks obstruct.

Think, when our one soul understands
   The great Word which makes all things new
When earth breaks up and heaven expands,
   How will the change strike me and you
In the house not made with hands?

Oh, I must feel your brain prompt mine,
   Your heart anticipate my heart,
You must be just before, in fine,
   See and make me see, for your part,
New depths of the divine!

But who could have expected this
   When we two drew together first
Just for the obvious human bliss,
   To satisfy life's daily thirst
With a thing men seldom miss?

Come back with me to the first of all,
   Let us lean and love it over again,

Let us now forget and now recall,
   Break the rosary in a pearly rain
And gather what we let fall!

What did I say?—that a small bird sings
   All day long, save when a brown pair
Of hawks from the wood float with wide wings
   Strained to a bell: 'gainst noon-day glare
You count the streaks and rings.

But at afternoon or almost eve
   'Tis better; then the silence grows
To that degree, you half believe
   It must get rid of what it knows,
Its bosom does so heave.

Hither we walked then, side by side,
   Arm in arm and cheek to cheek,
And still I questioned or replied,
   While my heart, convulsed to really speak,
Lay choking in its pride.

Silent the crumbling bridge we cross,
   And pity and praise the chapel sweet,
And care about the fresco's loss,
   And wish for our souls a like retreat,
And wonder at the moss.

Stoop and kneel on the settle under,
   Look through the window's grated square:

Nothing to see! For fear of plunder,
  The cross is down and the altar bare,
As if thieves don't fear thunder.

We stoop and look in through the grate,
  See the little porch and rustic door,
Read duly the dead builder's date;
  Then cross the bridge that we crossed before,
Take the path again—but wait!

Oh moment, one and infinite!
  The water slips o'er stock and stone;
The West is tender, hardly bright:
  How grey at once is the evening grown—
One star, its chrysolite!

We two stood there with never a third,
  But each by each, as each knew well:
The sights we saw and the sounds we heard,
  The lights and the shades made up a spell
Till the trouble grew and stirred.

Oh, the little more, and how much it is!
  And the little less, and what worlds away!
How a sound shall quicken content to bliss,
  Or a breath suspend the blood's best play,
And life be a proof of this!

Had she willed it, still had stood the screen
  So slight, so sure, 'twixt my love and her:

I could fix her face with a guard between,
And find her soul as when friends confer,
Friends—lovers that might have been.

For my heart had a touch of the woodland-time,
Wanting to sleep now over its best.
Shake the whole tree in the summer-prime,
But bring to the last leaf no such test!
"Hold the last fast!" runs the rhyme.

For a chance to make your little much,
To gain a lover and lose a friend,
Venture the tree and a myriad such,
When nothing you mar but the year can mend:
But a last leaf—fear to touch!

Yet should it unfasten itself and fall
Eddying down till it find your face
At some slight wind—best chance of all!
Be your heart henceforth its dwelling-place
You trembled to forestall!

Worth how well, those dark grey eyes,
That hair so dark and dear, how worth
That a man should strive and agonize,
And taste a veriest hell on earth
For the hope of such a prize!

You might have turned and tried a man,
Set him a space to weary and wear,

And prove which suited more your plan,
  His best of hope or his worst despair,
Yet end as he began.

But you spared me this, like the heart you are,
  And filled my empty heart at a word.
If two lives join, there is oft a scar,
  They are one and one, with a shadowy third;
One near one is too far.

A moment after, and hands unseen
  Were hanging the night around us fast;
But we knew that a bar was broken between
  Life and life: we were mixed at last
In spite of the mortal screen.

The forests had done it; there they stood;
  We caught for a moment the powers at play.
They had mingled us so, for once and good,
  Their work was done—we might go or stay,
They relapsed to their ancient mood.

How the world is made for each of us!
  How all we perceive and know in it
Tends to some moment's product thus,
  When a soul declares itself—to wit,
By its fruit, the thing it does!

Be hate that fruit or love that fruit,
   It forwards the general deed of man,
And each of the Many helps to recruit
   The life of the race by a general plan;
Each living his own, to boot.

I am named and known by that moment's feat,
   There took my station and degree;
So grew my own small life complete,
   As nature obtained her best of me—
One born to love you, sweet!

And to watch you sink by the fireside now
   Back again, as you mutely sit
Musing by fire-light, that great brow
   And the spirit-small hand propping it,
Yonder, my heart knows how!

So, earth has gained by one man the more,
   And the gain of earth must be heaven's gain too;
And the whole is well worth thinking o'er
   When autumn comes: which I mean to do
One day, as I said before.

Any Wife to Any Husband

MY love, this is the bitterest, that thou—
Who art all truth, and who dost love me now
    As thine eyes say, as thy voice breaks to say—
Shouldst love so truly, and couldst love me still
A whole long life through, had but love its will,
    Would death that leads me from thee brook delay.

I have but to be by thee, and thy hand
Will never let mine go, nor heart withstand
    The beating of my heart to reach its place.
When shall I look for thee and feel thee gone?
When cry for the old comfort and find none?
    Never, I know! Thy soul is in thy face.

Oh, I should fade—'tis willed so! Might I save,
Gladly I would, whatever beauty gave
    Joy to thy sense, for that was precious too.
It is not to be granted. But the soul
Whence the love comes, all ravage leaves that whole;
    Vainly the flesh fades; soul makes all things new.

It would not be because my eye grew dim
Thou couldst not find the love there, thanks to Him
    Who never is dishonored in the spark
He gave us from his fire of fires, and bade
Remember whence it sprang, nor be afraid
    While that burns on, though all the rest grow dark.

So, how thou wouldst be perfect, white and clean
Outside as inside, soul and soul's demesne

Alike, this body given to show it by!
Oh, three-parts through the worst of life's abyss,
What plaudits from the next world after this,
Couldst thou repeat a stroke and gain the sky!

And is it not the bitterer to think
That disengage our hands and thou wilt sink
Although thy love was love in very deed?
I know that nature! Pass a festive day,
Thou dost not throw its relic-flower away
Nor bid its music's loitering echo speed.

Thou let'st the stranger's glove lie where it fell;
If old things remain old things all is well,
For thou art grateful as becomes man best:
And hadst thou only heard me play one tune,
Or viewed me from a window, not so soon
With thee would such things fade as with the rest.

I seem to see! We meet and part; 'tis brief;
The book I opened keeps a folded leaf,
The very chair I sat on, breaks the rank;
That is a portrait of me on the wall—
Three lines, my face comes at so slight a call:
And for all this, one little hour to thank!

But now, because the hour through years was fixed,
Because our inmost beings met and mixed,
Because thou once hast loved me—wilt thou dare
Say to thy soul and Who may list beside,
"Therefore she is immortally my bride;
Chance cannot change my love, nor time impair.

"So, what if in the dusk of life that's left,
I, a tired traveller of my sun bereft,
Look from my path when, mimicking the same,
The fire-fly glimpses past me, come and gone?
—Where was it till the sunset? Where anon
It will be at the sunrise! What's to blame?"

Is it so helpful to thee? Canst thou take
The mimic up, nor, for the true thing's sake,
Put gently by such efforts at a beam?
Is the remainder of the way so long,
Thou need'st the little solace, thou the strong?
Watch out thy watch, let weak ones doze and dream!

Ah, but the fresher faces! "Is it true,"
Thou'lt ask, "some eyes are beautiful and new?
Some hair,—how can one choose but grasp such wealth?
And if a man would press his lips to lips
Fresh as the wilding hedge-rose-cup there slips
The dewdrop out of, must it be by stealth?

"It cannot change the love still kept for Her,
More than if such a picture I prefer
Passing a day with, to a room's bare side:
The painted form takes nothing she possessed,
Yet, while the Titian's Venus lies at rest,
A man looks. Once more, what is there to chide?"

So must I see, from where I sit and watch,
My own self sell myself, my hand attach

Its warrant to the very thefts from me—
Thy singleness of soul that made me proud,
Thy purity of heart I loved aloud,
Thy man's-truth I was bold to bid God see!

Love so, then, if thou wilt! Give all thou canst
Away to the new faces—disentranced,
(Say it and think it) obdurate no more:
Re-issue looks and words from the old mint,
Pass them afresh, no matter whose the print
Image and superscription once they bore!

Re-coin thyself and give it them to spend,—
It all comes to the same thing at the end,
Since mine thou wast, mine art and mine shalt be,
Faithful or faithless, sealing up the sum
Or lavish of my treasure, thou must come
Back to the heart's place here I keep for thee!

Only, why should it be with stain at all?
Why must I, 'twixt the leaves of coronal,
Put any kiss of pardon on thy brow?
Why need the other women know so much,
And talk together, "Such the look and such
The smile he used to love with, then as now!"

Might I die last and show thee! Should I find
Such hardship in the few years left behind,
If free to take and light my lamp, and go
Into thy tomb, and shut the door and sit,

Seeing thy face on those four sides of it
  The better that they are so blank, I know!

Why, time was what I wanted, to turn o'er
Within my mind each look, get more and more
  By heart each word, too much to learn at first:
And join thee all the fitter for the pause
'Neath the low doorway's lintel. That were cause
  For lingering, though thou calledst, if I durst!

And yet thou art the nobler of us two:
What dare I dream of, that thou canst not do,
  Outstripping my ten small steps with one stride?
I 'll say then, here's a trial and a task—
Is it to bear?—if easy, I'll not ask:
  Though love fail, I can trust on in thy pride.

Pride?—when those eyes forestall the life behind
The death I have to go through!—when I find,
  Now that I want thy help most, all of thee!
What did I fear? Thy love shall hold me fast
Until the little minute's sleep is past
  And I wake saved.—And yet it will not be!

Two in the Campagna

I WONDER do you feel to-day
  As I have felt since, hand in hand,
We sat down on the grass, to stray
  In spirit better through the land,
This morn of Rome and May?

For me, I touched a thought, I know,
  Has tantalized me many times,
(Like turns of thread the spiders throw
  Mocking across our path) for rhymes
To catch at and let go.

Help me to hold it! First it left
  The yellowing fennel, run to seed
There, branching from the brickwork's cleft,
  Some old tomb's ruin: yonder weed
Took up the floating weft,

Where one small orange cup amassed
  Five beetles,—blind and green they grope
Among the honey-meal: and last,
  Everywhere on the grassy slope
I traced it. Hold it fast!

The champaign with its endless fleece
  Of feathery grasses everywhere!
Silence and passion, joy and peace,
  An everlasting wash of air—
Rome's ghost since her decease.

Such life here, through such lengths of hours,
   Such miracles performed in play,
Such primal naked forms of flowers,
   Such letting nature have her way
While heaven looks from its towers!

How say you? Let us, O my dove,
   Let us be unashamed of soul,
As earth lies bare to heaven above!
   How is it under our control
To love or not to love?

I would that you were all to me,
   You that are just so much, no more.
Nor yours nor mine, nor slave nor free!
   Where does the fault lie? What the core
O' the wound, since wound must be?

I would I could adopt your will,
   See with your eyes, and set my heart
Beating by yours, and drink my fill
   At your soul's springs,—your part my part
In life, for good and ill.

No. I yearn upward, touch you close,
   Then stand away. I kiss your cheek,
Catch your soul's warmth,—I pluck the rose
   And love it more than tongue can speak—
Then the good minute goes.

Already how am I so far
   Out of that minute? Must I go
Still like the thistle-ball, no bar,
   Onward, whenever light winds blow,
Fixed by no friendly star?

Just when I seemed about to learn!
   Where is the thread now? Off again!
The old trick! Only I discern—
   Infinite passion, and the pain
Of finite hearts that yearn.

Misconceptions

THIS is a spray the Bird clung to,
    Making it blossom with pleasure,
Ere the high tree-top she sprung to,
    Fit for her nest and her treasure.
    Oh, what a hope beyond measure
Was the poor spray's, which the flying feet hung to,—
So to be singled out, built in, and sung to!

This is a heart the Queen leant on,
    Thrilled in a minute erratic,
Ere the true bosom she bent on,
    Meet for love's regal dalmatic.
    Oh, what a fancy ecstatic
Was the poor heart's, ere the wanderer went on—
Love to be saved for it, proffered to, spent on!

A Serenade at the Villa

THAT was I, you heard last night,
  When there rose no moon at all,
Nor, to pierce the strained and tight
  Tent of heaven, a planet small:
Life was dead and so was light.

Not a twinkle from the fly,
  Not a glimmer from the worm;
When the crickets stopped their cry,
  When the owls forebore a term,
You heard music; that was I.

Earth turned in her sleep with pain,
  Sultrily suspired for proof:
In at heaven and out again,
  Lightning! —where it broke the roof,
Bloodlike, some few drops of rain.

What they could my words expressed.
  O my love, my all, my one!
Singing helped the verses best,
  And when singing's best was done,
To my lute I left the rest.

So wore night; the East was grey,
  White the broad-faced hemlock-flowers:
There would be another day;
  Ere its first of heavy hours
Found me, I had passed away.

What became of all the hopes,
    Words and song and lute as well?
Say, this struck you—"When life gropes
    Feebly for the path where fell
Light last on the evening slopes,

"One friend in that path shall be,
    To secure my step from wrong;
One to count night day for me,
    Patient through the watches long,
Serving most with none to see."

Never say—as something bodes—
    "So, the worst has yet a worse!
When life halts 'neath double loads,
    Better the task-master's curse
Than such music on the roads!

"When no moon succeeds the sun,
    Nor can pierce the midnight's tent
Any star, the smallest one,
    While some drops, where lightning rent,
Show the final storm begun—

"When the fire-fly hides its spot,
    When the garden-voices fail
In the darkness thick and hot,—
    Shall another voice avail,
That shape be where these are not?

"Has some plague a longer lease,
    Proffering its help uncouth?
Can't one even die in peace?
    As one shuts one's eyes on youth,
Is that face the last one sees?"

Oh, how dark your villa was,
    Windows fast and obdurate!
How the garden grudged me grass
    Where I stood—the iron gate
Ground its teeth to let me pass!

One Way of Love

ALL June I bound the rose in sheaves.
Now, rose by rose, I strip the leaves
And strew them where Pauline may pass.
She will not turn aside? Alas!
Let them lie. Suppose they die?
The chance was they might take her eye.

How many a month I strove to suit
These stubborn fingers to the lute!
To-day I venture all I know.
She will not hear my music? So!
Break the string; fold music's wing:
Suppose Pauline had bade me sing!

My whole life long I learned to love.
This hour my utmost art I prove
And speak my passion—heaven or hell?
She will not give me heaven? 'Tis well!
Lose who may—I still can say,
Those who win heaven, blest are they!

Another Way of Love

JUNE was not over
  Though past the full,
And the best of her roses
  Had yet to blow,
  When a man I know
(But shall not discover,
  Since ears are dull,
And time discloses)
Turned him and said with a man's true air,
Half sighing a smile in a yawn, as 'twere,—
"If I tire of your June, will she greatly care?"

Well, dear, in-doors with you!
  True! serene deadness
Tries a man's temper.
  What's in the blossom
  June wears on her bosom?
Can it clear scores with you?
  Sweetness and redness,
  Eadem semper!
Go, let me care for it greatly or slightly!
If June mend her bower now, your hand left unsightly
By plucking the roses,—my June will do rightly.

And after, for pastime,
  If June be refulgent
With flowers in completeness,
  All petals, no prickles,
  Delicious as trickles
Of wine poured at mass-time,—

And choose One indulgent
To redness and sweetness:
Or if, with experience of man and of spider,
June use my June-lightning, the strong insect-ridder,
And stop the fresh film-work,—why, June will consider.

A Pretty Woman

THAT fawn-skin-dappled hair of hers,
 And the blue eye
 Dear and dewy,
And that infantine fresh air of hers!

To think men cannot take you, Sweet,
 And enfold you,
 Ay, and hold you,
And so keep you what they make you, Sweet!

You like us for a glance, you know—
 For a word's sake
 Or a sword's sake,
All's the same, whate'er the chance, you know,

And in turn we make you ours, we say—
 You and youth too,
 Eyes and mouth too,
All the face composed of flowers, we say.

All's our own, to make the most of, Sweet—
 Sing and say for,
 Watch and pray for,
Keep a secret or go boast of, Sweet!

But for loving, why, you would not, Sweet,
 Though we prayed you,
 Paid you, brayed you
In a mortar—for you could not, Sweet!

So, we leave the sweet face fondly there:
Be its beauty
Its sole duty!
Let all hope of grace beyond, lie there!

And while the face lies quiet there,
Who shall wonder
That I ponder
A conclusion? I will try it there.

As,—why must one, for the love foregone,
Scout mere liking?
Thunder-striking
Earth,—the heaven, we looked above for, gone!

Why, with beauty, needs there money be,
Love with liking?
Crush the fly-king
In his gauze, because no honey-bee?

May not liking be so simple-sweet,
If love grew there
'Twould undo there
All that breaks the cheek to dimples sweet?

Is the creature too imperfect, say?
Would you mend it
And so end it?
Since not all addition perfects aye!

Or is it of its kind, perhaps,
        Just perfection—
        Whence, rejection
Of a grace not to its mind, perhaps?

Shall we burn up, tread that face at once
        Into tinder,
        And so hinder
Sparks from kindling all the place at once?

Or else kiss away one's soul on her?
        Your love-fancies!
        —A sick man sees
Truer, when his hot eyes roll on her!

Thus the craftsman thinks to grace the rose,—
        Plucks a mould-flower
        For his gold flower,
Uses fine things that efface the rose:

Rosy rubies make its cup more rose,
        Precious metals
        Ape the petals,—
Last, some old king locks it up, morose!

Then how grace a rose? I know a way!
        Leave it, rather.
        Must you gather?
Smell, kiss, wear it—at last, throw away!

Respectability

DEAR, had the world in its caprice
    Deigned to proclaim "I know you both,
    Have recognized your plighted troth,
Am sponsor for you: live in peace!"—
How many precious months and years
    Of youth had passed, that speed so fast,
    Before we found it out at last,
The world, and what it fears!

How much of priceless life were spent
    With men that every virtue decks,
    And women models of their sex,
Society's true ornament,—
Ere we dared wander, nights like this,
    Through wind and rain, and watch the Seine,
    And feel the Boulevard break again
To warmth and light and bliss!

I know! the world proscribes not love;
    Allows my finger to caress
    Your lips' contour and downiness,
Provided it supply a glove.
The world's good word!—the Institute!
    Guizot receives Montalembert!
    Eh? Down the court three lampions flare:
Put forward your best foot!

Love in a Life

ROOM after room,
I hunt the house through
We inhabit together.
Heart, fear nothing, for, heart, thou shalt find her—
Next time, herself!—not the trouble behind her
Left in the curtain, the couch's perfume!
As she brushed it, the cornice-wreath blossomed anew:
Yon looking-glass gleamed at the wave of her feather.

Yet the day wears,
And door succeeds door;
I try the fresh fortune—
Range the wide house from the wing to the centre.
Still the same chance! she goes out as I enter.
Spend my whole day in the quest,—who cares?
But 'tis twilight, you see,—with such suites to explore,
Such closets to search, such alcoves to importune!

Life in a Love

ESCAPE me?
Never—
Beloved!
While I am I, and you are you,
So long as the world contains us both,
Me the loving and you the loth,
While the one eludes, must the other pursue.
My life is a fault at last, I fear:
It seems too much like a fate, indeed!
Though I do my best I shall scarce succeed.
But what if I fail of my purpose here?
It is but to keep the nerves at strain,
To dry one's eyes and laugh at a fall,
And baffled, get up and begin again,—
So the chase takes up one's life, that's all.
While, look but once from your farthest bound
At me so deep in the dust and dark,
No sooner the old hope goes to ground
Than a new one, straight to the selfsame mark,
I shape me—
Ever
Removed!

In Three Days

SO, I shall see her in three days
And just one night, but nights are short,
Then two long hours, and that is morn.
See how I come, unchanged, unworn!
Feel, where my life broke off from thine,
How fresh the splinters keep and fine,—
Only a touch and we combine!

Too long, this time of year, the days!
But nights, at least the nights are short.
As night shows where her one moon is,
A hand's-breadth of pure light and bliss,
So life's night gives my lady birth
And my eyes hold her! What is worth
The rest of heaven, the rest of earth?

O loaded curls, release your store
Of warmth and scent, as once before
The tingling hair did, lights and darks
Outbreaking into fairy sparks,
When under curl and curl I pried
After the warmth and scent inside,
Through lights and darks how manifold—
The dark inspired, the light controlled!
As early Art embrowns the gold.

What great fear, should one say, "Three days
That change the world might change as well

Your fortune; and if joy delays,
Be happy that no worse befell!"
What small fear, if another says,
"Three days and one short night beside
May throw no shadow on your ways;
But years must teem with change untried,
With chance not easily defied,
With an end somewhere undescried."
No fear! – or if a fear be born
This minute, it dies out in scorn.
Fear? I shall see her in three days
And one night, now the nights are short,
Then just two hours, and that is morn.

In a Year

NEVER any more,
  While I live,
Need I hope to see his face
  As before.
Once his love grown chill,
  Mine may strive:
Bitterly we re-embrace,
  Single still.

Was it something said,
  Something done,
Vexed him? Was it touch of hand,
  Turn of head?
Strange! that very way
  Love begun:
I as little understand
  Love's decay.

When I sewed or drew,
  I recall
How he looked as if I sung,
  —Sweetly too.
If I spoke a word,
  First of all
Up his cheek the color sprung,
  Then he heard.

Sitting by my side,
  At my feet,

So he breathed but air I breathed,
   Satisfied!
I, too, at love's brim
   Touched the sweet:
I would die if death bequeathed
   Sweet to him.

"Speak, I love thee best!"
   He exclaimed:
"Let thy love my own foretell!"
   I confessed:
"Clasp my heart on thine
   Now unblamed,
Since upon thy soul as well
   Hangeth mine!"

Was it wrong to own,
   Being truth?
Why should all the giving prove
   His alone?
I had wealth and ease,
   Beauty, youth:
Since my lover gave me love,
   I gave these.

That was all I meant,
   —To be just,
And the passion I had raised,
   To content.
Since he chose to change
   Gold for dust,

If I gave him what he praised
  Was it strange?

Would he loved me yet,
  On and on,
While I found some way undreamed
  —Paid my debt!
Gave more life and more,
  Till, all gone,
He should smile "She never seemed
  Mine before.

"What, she felt the while,
  Must I think?
Love's so different with us men!"
  He should smile:
"Dying for my sake—
  White and pink!
Can't we touch these bubbles then
  But they break?"

Dear, the pang is brief,
  Do thy part,
Have thy pleasure! How perplexed
  Grows belief!
Well, this cold clay clod
  Was man's heart:
Crumble it, and what comes next?
  Is it God?

Women and Roses

(Written on the suggestion of some roses sent Mrs. Browning. At the time of writing, Browning was carrying out a resolve to write a poem a day, a resolve which lasted a fortnight.)

I

I DREAM of a red-rose tree.
And which of its roses three
Is the dearest rose to me?

II

Round and round, like a dance of snow
In a dazzling drift, as its guardians, go
Floating the women faded for ages,
Sculptured in stone, on the poet's pages.
Then follow women fresh and gay,
Living and loving and loved to-day,
Last, in the rear, flee the multitude of maidens,
Beauties yet unborn. And all, to one cadence,
They circle their rose on my rose tree.

III

Dear rose, thy term is reached,
Thy leaf hangs loose and bleached:
Bees pass it unimpeached.

IV

Stay then, stoop, since I cannot climb,
You, great shapes of the antique time!
How shall I fix you, fire you, freeze you,
Break my heart at your feet to please you?
Oh, to possess and be possessed!
Hearts that beat 'neath each pallid breast!

Once but of love, the poesy, the passion,
Drink but once and die! — In vain, the same fashion,
They circle their rose on my rose tree.

V

Dear rose, thy joy's undimmed,
Thy cup is ruby-rimmed,
Thy cup's heart nectar-brimmed.

VI

Deep, as drops from a statue's plinth
The bee sucked in by the hyacinth,
So will I bury me while burning,
Quench like him at a plunge my yearning,
Eyes in your eyes, lips on your lips!
Fold me fast where the cincture slips,
Prison all my soul in eternities of pleasure,
Girdle me for once! But no — the old measure,
They circle their rose on my rose tree.

VII

Dear rose without a thorn,
Thy bud's the babe unborn:
First streak of a new morn.

VIII

Wings, lend wings for the cold, the clear!
What is far conquers what is near.
Roses will bloom nor want beholders,
Sprung from the dust where our flesh moulders,

What shall arrive with the cycle's change?
A novel grace and a beauty strange.
I will make an Eve, be the artist that began her,
Shaped her to his mind!—Alas! in like manner
They circle their rose on my rose tree.

The Statue and the Bust

THERE'S a palace in Florence, the world knows well,
And a statue watches it from the square,
And this story of both do our townsmen tell.

Ages ago, a lady there,
At the farthest window facing the East
Asked, "Who rides by with the royal air?"

The bridesmaids' prattle around her ceased;
She leaned forth, one on either hand;
They saw how the blush of the bride increased—

They felt by its beats her heart expand—
As one at each ear and both in a breath
Whispered, "The Great-Duke Ferdinand."

That selfsame instant, underneath,
The Duke rode past in his idle way,
Empty and fine like a swordless sheath.

Gay he rode, with a friend as gay,
Till he threw his head back—"Who is she?"
—"A bride the Riccardi brings home to-day."

Hair in heaps lay heavily
Over a pale brow spirit-pure—
Carved like the heart of the coal-black tree,

Crisped like a war-steed's encolure—
And vainly sought to dissemble her eyes
Of the blackest black our eyes endure,

And lo, a blade for a knight's emprise
Filled the fine empty sheath of a man,—
The Duke grew straightway brave and wise.

He looked at her, as a lover can;
She looked at him, as one who awakes:
The past was a sleep, and her life began.

Now, love so ordered for both their sakes,
A feast was held that selfsame night
In the pile which the mighty shadow makes.

(For Via Larga is three-parts light,
But the palace overshadows one,
Because of a crime, which may God requite!

To Florence and God the wrong was done,
Through the first republic's murder there
By Cosimo and his cursed son.)

The Duke (with the statue's face in the square)
Turned in the midst of his multitude
At the bright approach of the bridal pair.

Face to face the lovers stood
A single minute and no more,
While the bridegroom bent as a man subdued—

Bowed till his bonnet brushed the floor—
For the Duke on the lady a kiss conferred,
As the courtly custom was of yore.

In a minute can lovers exchange a word?
If a word did pass, which I do not think,
Only one out of a thousand heard.

That was the bridegroom. At day's brink
He and his bride were alone at last
In a bed chamber by a taper's blink.

Calmly he said that her lot was cast,
That the door she had passed was shut on her
Till the final catafalk repassed.

The world meanwhile, its noise and stir,
Through a certain window facing the East
She could watch like a convent's chronicler.

Since passing the door might lead to a feast,
And a feast might lead to so much beside,
He, of many evils, chose the least.

"Freely I choose too," said the bride—
"Your window and its world suffice,"
Replied the tongue, while the heart replied—

"If I spend the night with that devil twice,
May his window serve as my loop of hell
Whence a damned soul looks on paradise!

"I fly to the Duke who loves me well,
Sit by his side and laugh at sorrow
Ere I count another ave-bell.

" 'Tis only the coat of a page to borrow,
And tie my hair in a horse-boy's trim.
And I save my soul—but not to-morrow"—

(She checked herself and her eye grew dim)
"My father tarries to bless my state:
I must keep it one day more for him.

"Is one day more so long to wait?
Moreover the Duke rides past, I know;
We shall see each other, sure as fate."

She turned on her side and slept. Just so!
So we resolve on a thing and sleep:
So did the lady, ages ago.

That night the Duke said, "Dear or cheap
As the cost of this cup of bliss may prove
To body or soul, I will drain it deep."

And on the morrow, bold with love,
He beckoned the bridegroom (close on call,
As his duty bade, by the Duke's alcove)

And smiled " 'Twas a very funeral,
Your lady will think, this feast of ours,—
A shame to efface, whate'er befall!

"What if we break from the Arno bowers,
And try if Petraja, cool and green,
Cure last night's fault with this morning flowers?"

The bridegroom, not a thought to be seen
On his steady brow and quiet mouth,
Said, "Too much favor for me so mean!

"But, alas! my lady leaves the South;
Each wind that comes from the Apennine
Is a menace to her tender youth:

"Nor a way exists, the wise opine,
If she quits her palace twice this year,
To avert the flower of life's decline."

Quoth the Duke, "A sage and a kindly fear
Moreover Petraja is cold this spring:
Be our feast to-night as usual here!"

And then to himself—"Which night shall bring
Thy bride to her lover's embraces, fool—
Or I am the fool, and thou art the king!

"Yet my passion must wait a night, nor cool—
For to-night the Envoy arrives from France
Whose heart I unlock with thyself, my tool.

"I need thee still and might miss perchance.
To-day is not wholly lost, beside,
With its hope of my lady's countenance:

"For I ride—what should I do but ride?
And passing her palace, if I list,
May glance at its window—well betide!"

So said, so done: nor the lady missed
One ray that broke from the ardent brow,
Nor a curl of the lips where the spirit kissed.

Be sure that each renewed the vow,
No morrow's sun should arise and set
And leave them then as it left them now.

But next day passed, and next day yet,
With still fresh cause to wait one day more
Ere each leaped over the parapet.

And still, as love's brief morning wore,
With a gentle start, half smile, half sigh,
They found love not as it seemed before.

They thought it would work infallibly,
But not in despite of heaven and earth:
The rose would blow when the storm passed by.

Meantime they could profit in winter's dearth
By store of fruits that supplant the rose:
The world and its ways have a certain worth:

And to press a point while these oppose
Were simple policy; better wait:
We lose no friends and we gain no foes.

Meantime, worse fates than a lover's fate,
Who daily may ride and pass and look
Where his lady watches behind the grate!

And she—she watched the square like a book
Holding one picture and only one,
Which daily to find she undertook:

When the picture was reached the book was done,
And she turned from the picture at night to scheme
Of tearing it out for herself next sun.

So weeks grew months, years; gleam by gleam
The glory dropped from their youth and love,
And both perceived they had dreamed a dream;

Which hovered as dreams do, still above:
But who can take a dream for a truth?
Oh, hide our eyes from the next remove!

One day as the lady saw her youth
Depart, and the silver thread that streaked
Her hair, and, worn by the serpent's tooth,

The brow so puckered, the chin so peaked,—
And wondered who the woman was,
Hollow-eyed and haggard-cheeked,

Fronting her silent in the glass—
"Summon here," she suddenly said,
"Before the rest of my old self pass,

"Him, the Carver, a hand to aid,
Who fashions the clay no love will change,
And fixes a beauty never to fade.

"Let Robbia's craft so apt and strange
Arrest the remains of young and fair,
And rivet them while the seasons range.

"Make me a face on the window there,
Waiting as ever, mute the while,
My love to pass below in the square!

"And let me think that it may beguile
Dreary days which the dead must spend
Down in their darkness under the aisle,

"To say, 'What matters it at the end?
I did no more while my heart was warm
Than does that image, my pale-faced friend.'

"Where is the use of the lip's red charm,
The heaven of hair, the pride of the brow,
And the blood that blues the inside arm—

"Unless we turn, as the soul knows how,
The earthly gift to an end divine?
A lady of clay is as good, I trow."

But long ere Robbia's cornice, fine,
With flowers and fruits which leaves enlace,
Was set where now is the empty shrine—

(And, leaning out of a bright blue space,
As a ghost might lean from a chink of sky,
The passionate pale lady's face—

Eying ever, with earnest eye
And quick-turned neck at its breathless stretch
Some one who ever is passing by—)

The Duke has sighed like the simplest wretch
In Florence, "Youth—my dream escapes!
Will its record stay?" And he bade them fetch

Some subtle moulder of brazen shapes—
"Can the soul, the will, die out of a man
Ere his body find the grave that gapes?

"John of Douay shall effect my plan,
Set me on horseback here aloft,
Alive, as the crafty sculptor can,

"In the very square I have crossed so oft;
That men may admire, when future suns
Shall touch the eyes to a purpose soft,

"While the mouth and the brow stay brave in bronze—
Admire and say, 'When he was alive
How he would take his pleasure once!'

"And it shall go hard but I contrive
To listen the while, and laugh in my tomb
At idleness which aspires to strive."

So! While these wait the trump of doom,
How do their spirits pass, I wonder,
Nights and days in the narrow room?

Still, I suppose, they sit and ponder
What a gift life was, ages ago,
Six steps out of the chapel yonder.

Only they see not God, I know,
Nor all that chivalry of his,
The soldier-saints who, row on row,

Burn upward each to his point of bliss—
Since, the end of life being manifest,
He had burned his way through the world to this.

I hear you reproach, "But delay was best,
For their end was a crime."—Oh, a crime will do
As well, I reply, to serve for a test,

As a virtue golden through and through,
Sufficient to vindicate itself
And prove its worth at a moment's view!

Must a game be played for the sake of pelf?
Where a button goes, 'twere an epigram
To offer the stamp of the very Guelph.

The true has no value beyond the sham:
As well the counter as coin, I submit,
When your table's a hat, and your prize, a dram.

Stake your counter as boldly every whit,
Venture as warily, use the same skill,
Do your best, whether winning or losing it,

If you choose to play! — is my principle.
Let a man contend to the uttermost
For his life's set prize, be it what it will!

The counter our lovers staked was lost
As surely as if it were lawful coin:
And the sin I impute to each frustrate ghost

Is — the unlit lamp and the ungirt loin,
Though the end in sight was a vice, I say.
You of the virtue (we issue join)
How strive you? *De te, fabula!*

Porphyria's Lover

THE rain set early in to-night,
  The sullen wind was soon awake,
It tore the elm-tops down for spite,
  And did its worst to vex the lake:
I listened with heart fit to break.
When glided in Porphyria; straight
  She shut the cold out and the storm,
And kneeled and made the cheerless grate
  Blaze up, and all the cottage warm;
Which done, she rose, and from her form
Withdrew the dripping cloak and shawl,
  And laid her soiled gloves by, untied
Her hat and let the damp hair fall,
  And, last, she sat down by my side
And called me. When no voice replied,
She put my arm about her waist,
  And made her smooth white shoulder bare
And all her yellow hair displaced,
  And, stooping, made my cheek lie there,
And spread, o'er all, her yellow hair,
Murmuring how she loved me—she
  Too weak, for all her heart's endeavor,
To set its struggling passion free
  From pride, and vainer ties dissever,
And give herself to me forever.
But passion sometimes would prevail,
  Nor could to-night's gay feast restrain
A sudden thought of one so pale
  For love of her, and all in vain:
So, she was come through wind and rain.
Be sure I looked up at her eyes

Happy and proud; at last I knew
Porphyria worshipped me; surprise
Made my heart swell, and still it grew
While I debated what to do.
That moment she was mine, mine, fair,
Perfectly pure and good: I found
A thing to do, and all her hair
In one long yellow string I wound
Three times her little throat around,
And strangled her. No pain felt she;
I am quite sure she felt no pain.
As a shut bud that holds a bee,
I warily oped her lids: again
Laughed the blue eyes without a stain.
And I untightened next the tress
About her neck; her cheek once more
Blushed bright beneath my burning kiss:
I propped her head up as before,
Only, this time my shoulder bore
Her head, which droops upon it still:
The smiling rosy little head,
So glad it has its utmost will,
That all it scorned at once is fled,
And I, its love, am gained instead!
Porphyria's love: she guessed not how
Her darling one wish would be heard.
And thus we sit together now,
And all night long we have not stirred,
And yet God has not said a word!

James Lee's Wife

1

JAMES LEE'S WIFE SPEAKS AT THE WINDOW

AH, Love, but a day
    And the world has changed!
The sun's away,
    And the bird estranged;
The wind has dropped,
    And the sky's deranged:
Summer has stopped.

Look in my eyes!
    Wilt thou change too?
Should I fear surprise?
    Shall I find aught new
In the old and dear,
    In the good and true,
With the changing year?

Thou art a man,
    But I am thy love.
For the lake, its swan;
    For the dell its dove;
And for thee – (oh, haste!)
    Me, to bend above,
Me, to hold embraced.

2

BY THE FIRESIDE

Is all our fire of shipwreck wood,
    Oak and pine?

Oh, for the ills half-understood,
        The dim dead woe
        Long ago
Befallen this bitter coast of France!
Well, poor sailors took their chance;
        I take mine.

A ruddy shaft our fire must shoot
        O'er the sea:
Do sailors eye the casement—mute
        Drenched and stark,
        From their bark—
And envy, gnash their teeth for hate
O' the warm safe house and happy freight
        —Thee and me?

God help you, sailors, at your need!
        Spare the curse!
For some ships, safe in port indeed,
        Rot and rust,
        Run to dust,
All through worms i' the wood, which crept,
Gnawed our hearts out while we slept:
        That is worse.

Who lived here before us two?
        Old-world pairs.
Did a woman ever—would I knew!—
        Watch the man
        With whom began

Love's voyage full-sail,—(now gnash your teeth!)
When planks start, open hell beneath
Unawares?

3

IN THE DOORWAY

The swallow has set her six young on the rail,
And looks seaward:
The water's in stripes like a snake, olive-pale
To the leeward,—
On the weather-side, black, spotted white with the wind.
"Good fortune departs, and disaster's behind,"—
Hark, the wind with its wants and its infinite wail!

Our fig-tree, that leaned for the saltness, has furled
Her five fingers,
Each leaf like a hand opened wide to the world
Where there lingers
No glint of the gold, Summer sent for her sake:
How the vines writhe in rows, each impaled on its stake!
My heart shrivels up and my spirit shrinks curled.

Yet here are we two; we have love, house enough,
With the field there,
This house of four rooms, that field red and rough,
Though it yield there,
For the rabbit that robs, scarce a blade or a bent;
If a magpie alight now, it seems an event;
And they both will be gone at November's rebuff.

But why must cold spread? but wherefore bring change
    To the spirit.
God meant should mate his with an infinite range,
    And inherit
His power to put life in the darkness and cold?
Oh, live and love worthily, bear and be bold!
Whom Summer made friends of, let Winter estrange!

4

ALONG THE BEACH

I will be quiet and talk with you,
    And reason why you are wrong.
You wanted my love—is that much true?
And so I did love, so I do:
    What has come of it all along?

I took you—how could I otherwise?
    For a world to me, and more;
For all, love greatens and glorifies
Till God's aglow, to the loving eyes,
    In what was mere earth before.

Yes, earth—yes, mere ignoble earth!
    Now do I mis-state, mistake?
Do I wrong your weakness and call it worth?
Expect all harvest, dread no dearth,
    Seal my sense up for your sake?

Oh, Love, Love, no, Love! not so, indeed!
    You were just weak earth, I knew:

With much in you waste, with many a weed,
And plenty of passions run to seed,
   But a little good grain too.

And such as you were, I took you for mine:
   Did not you find me yours,
To watch the olive and wait the vine,
And wonder when rivers of oil and wine
   Would flow, as the Book assures?

Well, and if none of these good things came,
   What did the failure prove?
The man was my whole world, all the same,
With his flowers to praise or his weeds to blame,
   And, either or both, to love.

Yet this turns now to a fault—there! there!
   That I do love, watch too long,
And wait too well, and weary and wear;
And 'tis all an old story, and my despair
   Fit subject for some new song:

"How the light, light love, he has wings to fly
   At suspicion of a bond:
My wisdom has bidden your pleasure good-by,
Which will turn up next in a laughing eye,
   And why should you look beyond?"

5

ON THE CLIFF

I leaned on the turf,
I looked at a rock
Left dry by the surf;
For the turf, to call it grass were to mock:
Dead to the roots, so deep was done
The work of the summer sun.

And the rock lay flat
As an anvil's face:
No iron like that!
Baked dry; of a weed, of a shell, no trace:
Sunshine outside, but ice at the core,
Death's altar by the lone shore.

On the turf, sprang gay
With his films of blue,
No cricket, I'll say,
But a warhorse, barded and chanfroned too,
The gift of a quixote-mage to his knight,
Real fairy, with wings all right.

On the rock, they scorch
Like a drop of fire
From a brandished torch,
Fall two red fans of a butterfly:
No turf, no rock: in their ugly stead,
See, wonderful blue and red!

Is it not so
With the minds of men?
The level and low,
The burnt and bare, in themselves; but then
With such a blue and red grace, not theirs,—
Love settling unawares!

6

READING A BOOK, UNDER THE CLIFF

"Still ailing, Wind? Wilt be appeased or no?
  Which needs the other's office, thou or I?
Dost want to be disburdened of a woe,
  And can, in truth, my voice untie
Its links, and let it go?

"Art thou a dumb, wronged thing that would be righted,
  Entrusting thus thy cause to me? Forbear!
No tongue can mend such pleadings; faith, requited
  With falsehood,—love, at last aware
Of scorn,—hopes, early blighted,—

"We have them; but I know not any tone
  So fit as thine to falter forth a sorrow:
Dost think men would go mad without a moan,
  If they knew any way to borrow
A pathos like thy own?

"Which sigh wouldst mock, of all the sighs? The one
  So long escaping from lips starved and blue,

That lasts while on her pallet-bed the nun
   Stretches her length; her foot comes through
The straw she shivers on;

"You had not thought she was so tall and spent,
   Her shrunk lids open, her lean fingers shut
Close, close, their sharp and livid nails indent
   The clammy palm; then all is mute:
That way, the spirit went.

"Or wouldst thou rather that I understand
   Thy will to help me?—like the dog I found
Once, pacing sad this solitary strand,
   Who would not take my food, poor hound,
But whined and licked my hand."

All this, and more, comes from some young man's pride
   Of power to see,—in failure and mistake,
Relinquishment, disgrace, on every side,—
   Merely examples for his sake,
Helps to his path untried:

Instances he must—simply recognize?
   Oh, more than so!—must, with a learner's zeal,
Make doubly prominent, twice emphasize,
   By added touches that reveal
The god in babe's disguise.

Oh, he knows what defeat means, and the rest!
   Himself the undefeated that shall be:

Failure, disgrace, he flings them you to test,—
  His triumph, in eternity
Too plainly manifest!

Whence, judge if he learn forthwith what the wind
  Means in its moaning—by the happy prompt
Instinctive way of youth, I mean; for kind
  Calm years, exacting their accompt
Of pain, mature the mind:

And some midsummer morning, at the lull
  Just about daybreak, as he looks across
A sparkling foreign country, wonderful
  To the sea's edge for gloom and gloss,
Next minute must annul,—

Then, when the wind begins among the vines,
  So low, so low, what shall it say but this?
"Here is the change beginning, here the lines
  Circumscribe beauty, set to bliss
The limit time assigns."

Nothing can be as it has been before;
  Better, so call it, only not the same.
To draw one beauty into our hearts' core,
  And keep it changeless! such our claim;
So answered,—Nevermore!

Simple? Why this is the old woe o' the world;
  Tune, to whose rise and fall we live and die.

Rise with it, then! Rejoice that man is hurled
From change to change unceasingly,
His soul's wings never furled!

That's a new question; still replies the fact,
Nothing endures: the wind moans, saying so;
We moan in acquiescence: there's life's pact.
Perhaps probation—do *I* know?
God does: endure his act!

Only, for man, how bitter not to grave
On his soul's hands' palms one fair good wise thing
Just as he grasped it! For himself, death's wave;
While time first washes—ah, the sting!—
O'er all he'd sink to save.

7

AMONG THE ROCKS

Oh, good gigantic smile o' the brown old earth,
This autumn morning! How he sets his bones
To bask i' the sun, and thrusts out knees and feet
For the ripple to run over in its mirth;
Listening the while, where on the heap of stones
The white breast of the sea-lark twitters sweet.

That is the doctrine, simple, ancient, true;
Such is life's trial, as old earth smiles and knows.
If you loved only what were worth your love,

Love were clear gain, and wholly well for you:
  Make the low nature better by your throes!
Give earth yourself, go up for gain above!

8

BESIDE THE DRAWING-BOARD

I

"As like as a Hand to another Hand!"
  Whoever said that foolish thing,
Could not have studied to understand
  The councils of God in fashioning,
Out of the infinite love of his heart,
This Hand, whose beauty I praise, apart
From the world of wonder left to praise,
If I tried to learn the other ways
Of love in its skill, or love in its power.
  "As like as a Hand to another Hand:"
  Who said that, never took his stand,
Found and followed, like me, an hour,
The beauty in this,—how free, how fine
To fear, almost,—of the limit-line!
As I looked at this, and learned and drew,
  Drew and learned, and looked again,
While fast the happy minutes flew,
  Its beauty mounted into my brain,
  And a fancy seized me; I was fain
To efface my work, begin anew,
Kiss what before I only drew;
Ay, laying the red chalk 'twixt my lips,
  With soul to help if the mere lips failed,
  I kissed all right where the drawing ailed.

Kissed fast the grace that somehow slips
Still from one's soulless finger-tips.

II

'Tis a clay cast, the perfect thing,
From Hand live once, dead long ago:
Princess-like it wears the ring
To fancy's eye, by which we know
That here at length a master found
His match, a proud lone soul its mate,
As soaring genius sank to ground,
And pencil could not emulate
The beauty in this,—how free, how fine
To fear almost!—of the limit-line.
Long ago the god, like me
The worm, learned, each in our degree:
Looked and loved, learned and drew,
Drew and learned and loved again,
While fast the happy minutes flew,
Till beauty mounted into his brain
And on the finger which outvied
His art he placed the ring that's there,
Still by fancy's eye descried,
In token of a marriage rare:
For him on earth, his art's despair,
For him in heaven, his soul's fit bride.

III

Little girl with the poor coarse hand
I turned from to a cold clay cast—
I have my lesson, understand
The worth of flesh and blood at last!

Nothing but beauty in a Hand?
    Because he could not change the hue,
    Mend the lines and make them true
To this which met his soul's demand,—
    Would Da Vinci turn from you?
I hear him laugh my woes to scorn—
"The fool forsooth is all forlorn
Because the beauty, she thinks best,
Lived long ago or was never born,—
Because no beauty bears the test
In this rough peasant Hand! Confessed
'Art is null and study void!'
So sayest thou? So said not I,
Who threw the faulty pencil by,
And years instead of hours employed,
Learning the veritable use
Of flesh and bone and nerve beneath
Lines and hue of the outer sheath,
If haply I might reproduce
One motive of the powers profuse,
Flesh and bone and nerve that make
The poorest coarsest human hand
An object worthy to be scanned
A whole life long for their sole sake.
Shall earth and the cramped moment-space
Yield the heavenly crowning grace?
Now the parts and then the whole!
Who art thou, with stinted soul
And stunted body, thus to cry,
'I love,—shall that be life's strait dole?
I must live beloved or die!'
This peasant hand that spins the wool
And bakes the bread, why lives it on,

Poor and coarse with beauty gone,—
What use survives the beauty?" Fool!

Go, little girl with the poor coarse hand!
I have my lesson, shall understand.

9

ON DECK

There is nothing to remember in me,
  Nothing I ever said with a grace,
Nothing I did that you care to see,
  Nothing I was that deserves a place
In your mind, now I leave you, set you free.

Conceded! In turn, concede to me,
  Such things have been as a mutual flame.
Your soul's locked fast; but, love for a key,
  You might let it loose, till I grew the same
In your eyes, as in mine you stand: strange plea!

For then, then, what would it matter to me
  That I was the harsh, ill-favored one?
We both should be like as pea and pea;
  It was ever so since the world begun:
So, let me proceed with my reverie.

How strange it were if you had all me,
  As I have all you in my heart and brain,
You, whose least word brought gloom or glee,
  Who never lifted the hand in vain—
Will hold mine yet, from over the sea!

Strange, if a face, when you thought of me,
   Rose like your own face present now,
With eyes as dear in their due degree,
   Much such a mouth, and as bright a brow,
Till you saw yourself, while you cried " 'Tis She!"

Well, you may, you must, set down to me
   Love that was life, life that was love;
A tenure of breath at your lips' decree,
   A passion to stand as your thoughts approve,
A rapture to fall where your foot might be.

But did one touch of such love for me
   Come in a word or a look of yours,
Whose words and looks will, circling, flee
   Round me and round while life endures,—
Could I fancy "As I feel, thus feels He;"

Why, fade you might to a thing like me,
   And your hair grow these coarse hanks of hair,
Your skin, this bark of a gnarled tree,—
   You might turn myself!—should I know or care,
When I should be dead of joy, James Lee?

Andrea del Sarto

(*Called "The Faultless Painter"*)

BUT do not let us quarrel any more,
No, my Lucrezia; bear with me for once:
Sit down and all shall happen as you wish.
You turn your face, but does it bring your heart?
I'll work then for your friend's friend, never fear,
Treat his own subject after his own way,
Fix his own time, accept to his own price,
And shut the money into this small hand
When next it takes mine. Will it? tenderly?
Oh, I'll content him,—but to-morrow, Love;
I often am much wearier than you think,
This evening more than usual, and it seems
As if—forgive now—should you let me sit
Here by the window with your hand in mine
And look a half-hour forth on Fiesole,
Both of one mind, as married people use,
Quietly, quietly the evening through,
I might get up to-morrow to my work
Cheerful and fresh as ever. Let us try.
To-morrow, how you shall be glad for this!
Your soft hand is a woman of itself,
And mine the man's bared breast she curls inside.
Don't count the time lost, neither; you must serve
For each of the five pictures we require:
It saves a model. So! keep looking so—
My serpentining beauty, rounds on rounds!
—How could you ever prick those perfect ears,
Even to put the pearl there! oh, so sweet—
My face, my moon, my everybody's moon,

Which everybody looks on and calls his,
And, I suppose, is looked on by in turn,
While she looks—no one's: very dear, no less.
You smile? why, there's my picture ready made.
There's what we painters call our harmony!
A common greyness silvers everything,—
All in a twilight, you and I alike
—You, at the point of your first pride in me
(That's gone you know),—but I, at every point,
My youth, my hope, my art, being all toned down
To yonder sober pleasant Fiesole.
There's the bell clinking from the chapel-top;
That length of convent-wall across the way
Holds the trees safer, huddled more inside;
The last monk leaves the garden; days decrease,
And autumn grows, autumn in everything.
Eh? the whole seems to fall into a shape
As if I saw alike my work and self
And all that I was born to be and do,
A twilight-piece. Love, we are in God's hand.
How strange now, looks the life he makes us lead;
So free we seem, so fettered fast we are!
I feel he laid the fetter: let it lie!
This chamber for example—turn your head—
All that's behind us! You don't understand
Nor care to understand about my art,
But you can hear at least when people speak:
And that cartoon, the second from the door
—It is the thing, Love! so such things should be—
Behold Madonna!—I am bold to say.
I can do with my pencil what I know,
What I see, what at bottom of my heart
I wish for, if I ever wish so deep—

Do easily, too—when I say, perfectly.
I do not boast, perhaps: yourself are judge,
Who listened to the Legate's talk last week,
And just as much they used to say in France.
At any rate 'tis easy, all of it!
No sketches first, no studies, that's long past:
I do what many dream of, all their lives,
—Dream? strive to do, and agonize to do,
And fail in doing. I could count twenty such
On twice your fingers, and not leave this town,
Who strive—you don't know how the others strive
To paint a little thing like that you smeared
Carelessly passing with your robes afloat,—
Yet do much less, so much less, Someone says,
(I know his name, no matter)—so much less!
Well, less is more, Lucrezia: I am judged.
There burns a truer light of God in them,
In their vexed beating stuffed and stopped-up brain,
Heart, or whate'er else, than goes on to prompt
This low-pulsed forthright craftsman's hand of mine.
Their works drop groundward, but themselves, I know,
Reach many a time a heaven that's shut to me,
Enter and take their place there sure enough,
Though they come back and cannot tell the world
My works are nearer heaven, but I sit here.
The sudden blood of these men! at a word—
Praise them, it boils, or blame them, it boils too.
I, painting from myself and to myself,
Know what I do, am unmoved by men's blame
Or their praise either. Somebody remarks
Morello's outline there is wrongly traced,
His hue mistaken; what of that? or else,
Rightly traced and well ordered; what of that?

Speak as they please, what does the mountain care?
Ah, but a man's reach should exceed his grasp,
Or what's a heaven for? All is silver-grey
Placid and perfect with my art: the worse!
I know both what I want and what might gain,
And yet how profitless to know, to sigh
"Had I been two, another and myself,
Our head would have o'erlooked the world!" No doubt.
Yonder's a work now, of that famous youth
The Urbinate who died five years ago.
('Tis copied, George Vasari sent it me.)
Well, I can fancy how he did it all,
Pouring his soul, with kings and popes to see,
Reaching, that heaven might so replenish him,
Above and through his art—for it gives way
That arm is wrongly put—and there again—
A fault to pardon in the drawing's lines,
Its body, so to speak: its soul is right,
He means right—that, a child may understand.
Still, what an arm! and I could alter it:
But all the play, the insight and the stretch—
Out of me, out of me! And wherefore out?
Had you enjoined them on me, given me soul,
We might have risen to Rafael, I and you!
Nay, Love, you did give all I asked, I think—
More than I merit, yes, by many times.
But had you—oh, with the same perfect brow,
And perfect eyes, and more than perfect mouth,
And the low voice my soul hears, as a bird
The fowler's pipe and follows to the snare—
Had you, with these the same, but brought a mind!
Some women do so. Had the mouth there urged
"God and the glory! never care for gain.

The present by the future, what is that?
Live for fame, side by side with Agnolo!
Rafael is waiting: up to God all three!"
I might have done it for you. So it seems:
Perhaps not. All is as God over-rules.
Beside, incentives come from the soul's self;
The rest avail not. Why do I need you?
What wife had Rafael, or has Agnolo?
In this world, who can do a thing, will not;
And who would do it, cannot, I perceive:
Yet the will's somewhat—somewhat, too, the power—
And thus we half-men struggle. At the end,
God, I conclude, compensates, punishes.
'Tis safer for me, if the award be strict,
That I am something underrated here,
Poor this long while, despised, to speak the truth.
I dared not, do you know, leave home all day,
For fear of chancing on the Paris lords.
The best is when they pass and look aside;
But they speak sometimes; I must bear it all.
Well may they speak! That Francis, that first time,
And that long festal year at Fontainebleau!
I surely then could sometimes leave the ground,
Put on the glory, Rafael's daily wear,
In that humane great monarch's golden look,—
One finger in his beard or twisted curl
Over his mouth's good mark that made the smile,
One arm about my shoulder, round my neck,
The jingle of his gold chain in my ear,
I painting proudly with his breath on me,
All his court round him, seeing with his eyes,
Such frank French eyes, and such a fire of souls
Profuse, my hand kept plying by those hearts,—

And, best of all, this, this, this face beyond,
This in the background, waiting on my work,
To crown the issue with a last reward!
A good time, was it not, my kingly days?
And had you not grown restless . . . but I know—
'Tis done and past; 'twas right, my instinct said;
Too live the life grew, golden and not grey,
And I'm the weak-eyed bat no sun should tempt
Out of the grange whose four walls make his world.
How could it end in any other way?
You called me, and I came home to your heart.
The triumph was—to reach and stay there; since
I reached it ere the triumph, what is lost?
Let my hands frame your face in your hair's gold,
You beautiful Lucrezia that are mine!
"Rafael did this, Andrea painted that;
The Roman's is the better when you pray,
But still the other's Virgin was his wife—"
Men will excuse me. I am glad to judge
Both pictures in your presence; clearer grows
My better fortune, I resolve to think.
For, do you know, Lucrezia, as God lives,
Said one day Agnolo, his very self,
To Rafael . . . I have known it all these years . . .
(When the young man was flaming out his thoughts
Upon a palace-wall for Rome to see,
Too lifted up in heart because of it)
"Friend, there's a certain sorry little scrub
Goes up and down our Florence, none cares how,
Who, were he set to plan and execute
As you are, pricked on by your popes and kings,
Would bring the sweat into that brow of yours!"
To Rafael's!—And indeed the arm is wrong.

I hardly dare . . . yet, only you to see,
Give the chalk here—quick, thus the line should go!
Ay, but the soul! he's Rafael! rub it out!
Still, all I care for, if he spoke the truth,
(What he? why, who but Michel Agnolo?
Do you forget already words like those?)
If really there was such a chance, so lost,—
Is, whether you're—not grateful—but more pleased.
Well, let me think so. And you smile indeed!
This hour has been an hour! Another smile?
If you would sit thus by me every night
I should work better, do you comprehend?
I mean that I should earn more, give you more.
See, it is settled dusk now; there's a star;
Morello's gone, the watch-lights show the wall.
The cue-owls speak the name we call them by.
Come from the window, love,—come in, at last,
Inside the melancholy little house
We built to be so gay with. God is just.
King Francis may forgive me: oft at nights
When I look up from painting, eyes tired out,
The walls become illumined, brick from brick
Distinct, instead of mortar, fierce bright gold,
That gold of his I did cement them with!
Let us but love each other. Must you go?
That Cousin here again? he waits outside?
Must see you—you, and not with me? Those loans?
More gaming debts to pay? you smiled for that?
Well, let smiles buy me! have you more to spend?
While hand and eye and something of a heart
Are left me, work's my ware, and what's it worth?
I'll pay my fancy. Only let me sit
The grey remainder of the evening out,

Idle, you call it, and muse perfectly
How I could paint, were I but back in France,
One picture, just one more—the Virgin's face,
Not yours this time! I want you at my side
To hear them—that is, Michel Agnolo—
Judge all I do and tell you of its worth.
Will you? To-morrow, satisfy your friend.
I take the subjects for his corridor,
Finish the portrait out of hand—there, there
And throw him in another thing or two
If he demurs; the whole should prove enough
To pay for this same Cousin's freak. Beside,
What's better and what's all I care about,
Get you the thirteen scudi for the ruff!
Love, does that please you? Ah, but what does he,
The Cousin! what does he to please you more?

I am grown peaceful as old age to-night.
I regret little, I would change still less.
Since there my past life lies, why alter it?
The very wrong to Francis!—it is true
I took his coin, was tempted and complied.
And built this house and sinned, and all is said.
My father and my mother died of want.
Well, had I riches of my own? you see
How one gets rich! Let each one bear his lot.
They were born poor, lived poor, and poor they died:
And I have laboured somewhat in my time
And not been paid profusely. Some good son
Paint my two hundred pictures—let him try!
No doubt, there's something strikes a balance. Yes,
You loved me quite enough, it seems to-night.

This must suffice me here. What would one have?
In heaven, perhaps, new chances, one more chance—
Four great walls in the New Jerusalem,
Meted on each side by the angel's reed,
For Leonard, Rafael, Agnolo and me
To cover—the three first without a wife,
While I have mine! So—still they overcome
Because there's still Lucrezia—as I choose.

Again the Cousin's whistle! Go, my Love.

Summum Bonum

ALL the breath and the bloom of the year in the bag of one bee:
All the wonder and wealth of the mine in the heart of one gem:
In the core of one pearl all the shade and the shine of the sea:
Breath and bloom, shade and shine,—wonder, wealth, and—how far above them—
Truth, that's brighter than gem,
Trust, that's purer than pearl,—
Brightest truth, purest trust in the universe—all were for me
In the kiss of one girl.

A Pearl, a Girl

A SIMPLE ring with a single stone,
  To the vulgar eye no stone of price:
Whisper the right word, that alone—
  Forth starts a sprite, like fire from ice,
And lo, you are lord (says an Eastern scroll)
Of heaven and earth, lord whole and sole
  Through the power in a pearl.

A woman ('tis I this time that say)
  With little the world counts worthy praise
Utter the true word—out and away
  Escapes her soul: I am wrapt in blaze,
Creation's lord, of heaven and earth
Lord whole and sole—by a minute's birth—
  Through the love in a girl!

Speculative

OTHERS may need new life in Heaven—
  Man, Nature, Art—made new, assume!
Man with new mind old sense to leaven,
  Nature,—new light to clear old gloom,
Art that breaks bounds, gets soaring-room.

I shall pray: "Fugitive as precious—
  Minutes which passed,—return, remain!
Let earth's old life once more enmesh us,
  You with old pleasure, me—old pain,
So we but meet nor part again!"

Bad Dreams

LAST night I saw you in my sleep:
  And how your charm of face was changed!
I asked, "Some love, some faith you keep?"
  You answered, "Faith gone, love estranged."

Whereat I woke—a twofold bliss:
  Waking was one, but next there came
This other: "Though I felt, for this,
  My heart break, I loved on the same."

Now

OUT of your whole life give but a moment!
All of your life that has gone before,
All to come after it,—so you ignore,
So you make perfect the present,—condense,
In a rapture of rage, for perfection's endowment,
Thought and feeling and soul and sense—
Merged in a moment which gives me at last
You around me for once, you beneath me, above me—
Me—sure that despite of time future, time past,—
This tick of our life-time's one moment you love me!
How long such suspension may linger? Ah, Sweet—
The moment eternal—just that and no more—
When ecstasy's utmost we clutch at the core
While cheeks burn, arms open, eyes shut and lips meet!

Humility

WHAT girl but, having gathered flowers,
Stript the beds and spoilt the bowers,
From the lapful light she carries
Drops a careless bud?—nor tarries
To regain the waif and stray:
"Store enough for home"—she'll say.

So say I too: give your lover
Heaps of loving—under, over,
Whelm him—make the one the wealthy!
Am I all so poor who—stealthy
Work it was!—picked up what fell:
Not the worst bud—who can tell?

Poetics

"SO say the foolish!" Say the foolish so, Love?
"Flower she is, my rose"—or else, "My very swan is she"—
Or perhaps, "Yon maid-moon, blessing earth below, Love,
That art thou!"—to them, belike: no such vain words from me.

"Hush, rose, blush! no balm like breath," I chide it:
"Bend thy neck its best, swan,—hers the whiter curve!"
Be the moon the moon: my Love I place beside it:
What is she? Her human self,—no lower word will serve.

Wanting Is—What?

WANTING is—what?
Summer redundant,
Blueness abundant,
—Where is the blot?
Beamy the world, yet a blank all the same,
—Framework which waits for a picture to frame:
What of the leafage, what of the flower?
Roses embowering with naught they embower!
Come then, complete incompletion, O comer,
Pant through the blueness, perfect the summer!
Breathe but one breath
Rose-beauty above,
And all that was death
Grows life, grows love,
Grows love!

Appearances

AND so you found that poor room dull,
  Dark, hardly to your taste, my dear?
Its features seemed unbeautiful:
  But this I know—'twas there, not here,
You plighted troth to me, the word
Which—ask that poor room how it heard.

And this rich room obtains your praise
  Unqualified,—so bright, so fair,
So all whereat perfection stays?
  Ay, but remember—here, not there,
The other word was spoken!—Ask
This rich room how you dropped the mask!

St. Martin's Summer

NO protesting, dearest!
Hardly kisses even!
Don't we both know how it ends?
How the greenest leaf turns serest,
Bluest outbreak—blankest heaven,
Lovers—friends?

You would build a mansion,
I would weave a bower
—Want the heart for enterprise.
Walls admit of no expansion:
Trellis-work may haply flower
Twice the size.

What makes glad Life's Winter?
New buds, old blooms after.
Sad the sighing "How suspect
Beams would ere mid-Autumn splinter,
Rooftree scarce support a rafter,
Walls lie wrecked?"

You are young, my princess!
I am hardly older:
Yet—I steal a glance behind!
Dare I tell you what convinces
Timid me that you, if bolder,
Bold—are blind?

Where we plan our dwelling
Glooms a graveyard surely!

Headstone, footstone moss may drape,—
Name, date, violets hide from spelling,—
But, though corpses rot obscurely,
Ghosts escape.

Ghosts! O breathing Beauty,
Give my frank word pardon!
What if I—somehow, somewhere—
Pledged my soul to endless duty
Many a time and oft? Be hard on
Love—laid there?

Nay, blame grief that's fickle,
Time that proves a traitor,
Chance, change, all that purpose warps,—
Death who spares to thrust the sickle
Laid Love low, through flowers which later
Shroud the corpse!

And you, my winsome lady,
Whisper with like frankness!
Lies nothing buried long ago?
Are yon—which shimmer 'mid the shady
Where moss and violet run to rankness—
Tombs or no?

Who taxes you with murder?
My hands are clean—or nearly!
Love being mortal needs must pass.
Repentance? Nothing were absurder.
Enough: we felt Love's loss severely;
Though now—alas!

Love's corpse lies quiet therefore,
Only Love's ghost plays truant,
And warns us have in wholesome awe
Durable mansionry; that's wherefore
I weave but trellis-work, pursuant
—Life, to law.

The solid, not the fragile,
Tempts rain and hail and thunder.
If bower stand firm at Autumn's close,
Beyond my hope,—why, boughs were agile;
If bower fall flat, we scarce need wonder
Wreathing—rose!

So, truce to the protesting,
So, muffled be the kisses!
For, would we but avow the truth,
Sober is genuine joy. No jesting!
Ask else Penelope, Ulysses—
Old in youth!

For why should ghosts feel angered?
Let all their interference
Be faint march-music in the air!
"Up! Join the rear of us the vanguard!
Up, lovers, dead to all appearance,
Laggard pair!"

The while you clasp me closer,
The while I press you deeper,
As safe we chuckle,—under breath,

Yet all the slyer, the jocoser,—
"So, life can boast its day, like leap-year,
Stolen from death!"

Ah me—the sudden terror!
Hence quick—avaunt, avoid me,
You cheat, the ghostly flesh-disguised!
Nay, all the ghosts in one! Strange error!
So, 'twas Death's self that clipped and coyed me,
Loved—and lied!

Ay, dead loves are the potent!
Like any cloud they used you,
Mere semblance you, but substance they!
Build we no mansion, weave we no tent!
Mere flesh—their spirit interfused you!
Hence, I say!

All theirs, none yours the glamour!
Theirs each low word that won me,
Soft look that found me Love's, and left
What else but you—the tears and clamor
That's all your very own! Undone me—
Ghost-bereft!

Magical Nature

FLOWER—I never fancied, jewel—I profess you!
  Bright I see and soft I feel the outside of a flower.
Save but glow inside and—jewel, I should guess you,
  Dim to sight and rough to touch: the glory is the dower.

You, forsooth, a flower? Nay, my love, a jewel—
  Jewel at no mercy of a moment in your prime!
Time may fray the flower-face: kind be time or cruel,
  Jewel, from each facet, flash your laugh at time!

Muckle-mouth Meg

FROWNED the Laird on the Lord: "So, red-handed I catch thee?
Death-doomed by our Law of the Border!
We've a gallows outside and a chiel to dispatch thee:
Who trespasses—hangs: all's in order."

He met frown with smile, did the young English gallant:
Then the Laird's dame: "Nay, Husband, I beg!
He's comely: be merciful! Grace for the callant
—If he marries our Muckle-mouth Meg!

"No mile-wide-mouthed monster of yours do I marry:
Grant rather the gallows!" laughed he.
"Foul fare kith and kin of you—why do you tarry?"
"To tame your fierce temper!" quoth she.

"Shove him quick in the Hole, shut him fast for a week:
Cold, darkness, and hunger work wonders:
Who lion-like roars now, mouse-fashion will squeak,
And 'it rains' soon succeed to 'it thunders.' "

A week did he bide in the cold and the dark
—Not hunger: for duly at morning
In flitted a lass, and a voice like a lark
Chirped, "Muckle-mouth Meg still ye're scorning?

"Go hang, but here's parritch to hearten ye first!"
"Did Meg's muckle-mouth boast within some
Such music as yours, mine should match it or burst:
No frog-jaws! So tell folk, my Winsome!"

Soon week came to end, and, from Hole's door set wide,
  Out he marched, and there waited the lassie:
"Yon gallows, or Muckle-mouth Meg for a bride!
  Consider! Sky's blue and turf's grassy:

"Life's sweet: shall I say ye wed Muckle-mouth Meg?"
  "Not I," quoth the stout heart: "too eerie
The mouth that can swallow a bubblyjock's egg;
  Shall I let it munch mine? Never, Dearie!

"Not Muckle-mouth Meg? Wow, the obstinate man!
  Perhaps he would rather wed me!"
"Ay, would he—with just for a dowry your can!"
  "I'm Muckle-mouth Meg," chirruped she.

"Then so—so—so—so—" as he kissed her apace—
  "Will I widen thee out till thou turnest
From Margaret Minnikin-mou', by God's grace,
  To Muckle-mouth Meg in good earnest!"

Youth and Art

IT once might have been, once only:
We lodged in a street together,
You, a sparrow on the housetop lonely,
I, a lone she-bird of his feather.

Your trade was with sticks and clay,
You thumbed, thrust, patted and polished,
Then laughed "They will see some day
Smith made, and Gibson demolished."

My business was song, song, song;
I chirped, cheeped, trilled and twittered,
"Kate Brown's on the boards ere long,
And Grisi's existence embittered!"

I earned no more by a warble
Than you by a sketch in plaster;
You wanted a piece of marble,
I needed a music-master.

We studied hard in our styles,
Chipped each at a crust like Hindoos,
For air, looked out on the tiles,
For fun, watched each other's windows.

You lounged, like a boy of the South,
Cap and blouse—nay, a bit of beard too;
Or you got it, rubbing your mouth
With fingers the clay adhered to.

And I—soon managed to find
  Weak points in the flower-fence facing,
Was forced to put up a blind
  And be safe in my corset-lacing.

No harm! It was not my fault
  If you never turned your eye's tail up
As I shook upon E *in alt.*,
  Or ran the chromatic scale up:

For spring bade the sparrows pair,
  And the boys and girls gave guesses,
And stalls in our street looked rare
  With bulrush and watercresses.

Why did not you pinch a flower
  In a pellet of clay and fling it?
Why did not I put a power
  Of thanks in a look, or sing it?

I did look, sharp as a lynx,
  (And yet the memory rankles,)
When models arrived, some minx
  Tripped up-stairs, she and her ankles.

But I think I gave you as good!
  "That foreign fellow,—who can know
How she pays, in a playful mood,
  For his tuning her that piano?"

Could you say so, and never say,
  "Suppose we join hands and fortunes,
And I fetch her from over the way,
  Her, piano, and long tunes and short tunes?"

No, no: you would not be rash,
  Nor I rasher and something over:
You've to settle yet Gibson's hash,
  And Grisi yet lives in clover.

But you meet the Prince at the Board,
  I'm queen myself at *bals-paré*,
I've married a rich old lord,
  And you're dubbed knight and an R.A.

Each life unfulfilled, you see;
  It hangs still, patchy and scrappy:
We have not sighed deep, laughed free,
  Starved, feasted, despaired,—been happy.

And nobody calls you a dunce,
  And people suppose me clever:
This could but have happened once,
  And we missed it, lost it for ever.

The Worst of It

WOULD it were I had been false, not you!
  I that am nothing, not you that are all:
I, never the worse for a touch or two
  On my speckled hide; not you, the pride
Of the day, my swan, that a first fleck's fall
  On her wonder of white must unswan, undo!

I had dipped in life's struggle and, out again,
  Bore specks of it here, there, easy to see,
When I found my swan and the cure was plain;
  The dull turned bright as I caught your white
On my bosom: you saved me—saved in vain
  If you ruined yourself, and all through me!

Yes, all through the speckled beast that I am,
  Who taught you to stoop; you gave me yourself,
And bound your soul by the vows that damn:
  Since on better thought you break, as you ought,
Vows—words, no angel set down, some elf
  Mistook,—for an oath, an epigram!

Yes, might I judge you, here were my heart,
  And a hundred its like, to treat as you pleased!
I choose to be yours, for my proper part,
  Yours, leave or take, or mar me or make;
If I acquiesce, why should you be teased
  With the conscience-prick and the memory-smart?

But what will God say? Oh, my sweet,
  Think, and be sorry you did this thing!
Though earth were unworthy to feel your feet,
  There's a heaven above may deserve your love:
Should you forfeit heaven for a snapt gold ring
  And a promise broke, were it just or meet?

And I to have tempted you! I, who tried
  Your soul, no doubt, till it sank! Unwise,
I loved, and was lowly, loved and aspired,
  Loved, grieving or glad, till I made you mad,
And you meant to have hated and despised—
  Whereas, you deceived me nor inquired!

She, ruined? How? No heaven for her?
  Crowns to give, and none for the brow
That looked like marble and smelt like myrrh?
  Shall the robe be worn, and the palm-branch borne,
And she go graceless, she graced now
  Beyond all saints, as themselves aver?

Hardly! That must be understood!
  The earth is your place of penance, then;
And what will it prove? I desire your good,
  But, plot as I may, I can find no way
How a blow should fall, such as falls on men,
  Nor prove too much for your womanhood.

It will come, I suspect, at the end of life,
  When you walk alone, and review the past;
And I, who so long shall have done with strife,
  And journeyed my stage and earned my wage

And retired as was right,—I am called at last
  When the devil stabs you, to lend the knife.

He stabs for the minute of trivial wrong,
  Nor the other hours are able to save,
The happy, that lasted my whole life long:
  For a promise broke, not for first words spoke,
The true, the only, that turn my grave
  To a blaze of joy and a crash of song.

Witness beforehand! Off I trip
  On a safe path gay through the flowers you flung:
My very name made great by your lip,
  And my heart aglow with the good I know
Of a perfect year when we both were young,
  And I tasted the angels' fellowship.

And witness, moreover . . . Ah, but wait!
  I spy the loop whence an arrow shoots!
It may be for yourself, when you meditate,
  That you grieve—for slain ruth, murdered truth:
"Though falsehood escape in the end, what boots?
  How truth would have triumphed!"—you sigh too late.

Ay, who would have triumphed like you, I say!
  Well, it is lost now; well, you must bear,
Abide and grow fit for a better day:
  You should hardly grudge, could I be your judge!
But hush! For you, can be no despair:
  There's amends: 'tis a secret: hope and pray!

For I was true at least—oh, true enough!
  And, Dear, truth is not as good as it seems!
Commend me to conscience! Idle stuff!
  Much help is in mine, as I mope and pine,
And skulk through day, and scowl in my dreams
  At my swan's obtaining the crow's rebuff.

Men tell me of truth now—"False!" I cry:
  Of beauty—"A mask, friend! Look beneath!"
We take our own method, the devil and I,
  With pleasant and fair and wise and rare:
And the best we wish to what lives, is—death;
  Which even in wishing, perhaps we lie!

Far better commit a fault and have done—
  As you, Dear!—forever; and choose the pure,
And look where the healing waters run,
  And strive and strain to be good again,
And a place in the other world ensure,
  All glass and gold, with God for its sun.

Misery! What shall I say or do?
  I cannot advise, or, at least, persuade:
Most like, you are glad you deceived me—rue
  No whit of the wrong: you endured too long,
Have done no evil and want no aid,
  Will live the old life out and chance the new.

And your sentence is written all the same,
  And I can do nothing,—pray, perhaps:
But somehow the world pursues its game,—
  If I pray, if I curse,—for better or worse:

And my faith is torn to a thousand scraps,
  And my heart feels ice while my words breathe flame.

Dear, I look from my hiding-place.
  Are you still so fair? Have you still the eyes?
Be happy! Add but the other grace,
  Be good! Why want what the angels vaunt?
I knew you once: but in Paradise,
  If we meet, I will pass nor turn my face.

Too Late

HERE was I with my arm and heart
  And brain, all yours for a word, a want
Put into a look—just a look, your part,—
  While mine, to repay it . . . vainest vaunt
Were the woman, that's dead, alive to hear,
  Had her lover, that's lost, love's proof to show!
But I cannot show it; you cannot speak
  From the churchyard neither, miles removed,
Though I feel by a pulse within my cheek,
  Which stabs and stops, that the woman I loved
Needs help in her grave and finds none near,
  Wants warmth from the heart which sends it—so!

Did I speak once angrily, all the drear days
  You lived, you woman I loved so well,
Who married the other? Blame or praise,
  Where was the use then? Time would tell,
And the end declare what man for you,
  What woman for me, was the choice of God.
But, Edith dead! no doubting more!
  I used to sit and look at my life
As it rippled and ran till, right before,
  A great stone stopped it: oh, the strife
Of waves at the stone some devil threw
  In my life's midcurrent, thwarting God!

But either I thought, "They may churn and chide
  Awhile, my waves which came for their joy
And found this horrible stone full-tide:
  Yet I see just a thread escape, deploy

Through the evening-country, silent and safe,
And it suffers no more till it finds the sea."
Or else I would think, "Perhaps some night
When new things happen, a meteor-ball
May slip through the sky in a line of light,
And earth breathe hard, and landmarks fall,
And my waves no longer champ nor chafe,
Since a stone will have rolled from its place: let be!"

But, dead! All's done with: wait who may,
Watch and wear and wonder who will.
Oh, my whole life that ends to-day!
Oh, my soul's sentence, sounding still,
"The woman is dead that was none of his;
And the man that was none of hers may go!"
There's only the past left: worry that!
Wreak, like a bull, on the empty coat,
Rage, its late wearer is laughing at!
Tear the collar to rags, having missed his throat;
Strike stupidly on—"This, this and this,
Where I would that a bosom received the blow!"

I ought to have done more: once my speech,
And once your answer, and there, the end,
And Edith was hencefortn out of reach!
Why, men do more to deserve a friend,
Be rid of a foe, get rich, grow wise,
Nor, folding their arms, stare fate in the face.
Why, better even have burst like a thief
And borne you away to a rock for us two,
In a moment's horror, bright, bloody and brief,
Then changed to myself again—"I slew

Myself in that moment; a ruffian lies
  Somewhere: your slave, see, born in his place!"

What did the other do? You be judge!
  Look at us, Edith! Here are we both!
Give him his six whole years: I grudge
  None of the life with you, nay, loathe
Myself that I grudged his start in advance
  Of me who could overtake and pass.
But, as if he loved you! No, not he,
  Nor any one else in the world, 'tis plain:
Who ever heard that another, free
  As I, young, prosperous, sound and sane,
Poured life out, proffered it—"Half a glance
  Of those eyes of yours and I drop the glass!"

Handsome, were you? 'Tis more than they held,
  More than they said; I was 'ware and watched:
I was the scapegrace, this rat belled
  The cat, this fool got his whiskers scratched:
The others? No head that was turned, no heart
  Broken, my lady, assure yourself!
Each soon made his mind up; so and so
  Married a dancer, such and such
Stole his friend's wife, stagnated slow,
  Or maundered, unable to do as much,
And muttered of peace where he had no part:
  While, hid in the closet, laid on the shelf,—

On the whole, you were let alone, I think!
  So, you looked to the other, who acquiesced;

My rival, the proud man,—prize your pink
  Of poets! A poet he was! I've guessed:
He rhymed you his rubbish nobody read,
  Loved you and loved you—did not I laugh!
There was a prize! But we both were tried.
  Oh, heart of mine, marked broad with her mark,
Tekel, found wanting, set aside,
  Scorned! See, I bleed these tears in the dark
Till comfort come and the last be bled:
  He? He is tagging your epitaph.

If it would only come over again!
  —Time to be patient with me, and probe
This heart till you punctured the proper vein,
  Just to learn what blood is: twitch the robe
From that blank lay-figure your fancy draped,
  Prick the leathern heart till the—verses spirt!
And late it was easy; late, you walked
  Where a friend might meet you; Edith's name
Arose to one's lip if one laughed or talked;
  If I heard good news, you heard the same;
When I woke, I knew that your breath escaped;
  I could bide my time, keep alive, alert.

And alive I shall keep and long, you will see!
  I knew a man, was kicked like a dog
From gutter to cesspool; what cared he
  So long as he picked from the filth his prog?
He saw youth, beauty and genius die,
  And jollily lived to his hundredth year.
But I will live otherwise: none of such life!
  At once I begin as I mean to end.

Go on with the world, get gold in its strife,
  Give your spouse the slip and betray your friend!
There are two who decline, a woman and I,
  And enjoy our death in the darkness here.

I liked that way you had with your curls
  Wound to a ball in a net behind:
Your cheek was chaste as a Quaker-girl's,
  And your mouth—there was never, to my mind,
Such a funny mouth, for it would not shut;
  And the dented chin too—what a chin!
There were certain ways when you spoke, some words
  That you know you never could pronounce:
You were thin, however; like a bird's
  Your hand seemed—some would say, the pounce
Of a scaly-footed hawk—all but!
  The world was right when it called you thin.

But I turn my back on the world: I take
  Your hand, and kneel, and lay to my lips.
Bid me live, Edith! Let me slake
  Thirst at your presence! Fear no slips:
'Tis your slave shall pay, while his soul endures,
  Full due, love's whole debt, *summum jus*.
My queen shall have high observance, planned
  Courtship made perfect, no least line
Crossed without warrant. There you stand,
  Warm too, and white too: would this wine
Had washed all over that body of yours.
  Ere I drank it, and you down with it, thus!

Confessions

WHAT is he buzzing in my ears?
"Now that I come to die,
Do I view the world as a vale of tears?"
Ah, reverend sir, not I!

What I viewed there once, what I view again
Where the physic bottles stand
On the table's edge,—is a suburb lane,
With a wall to my bedside hand.

That lane sloped, much as the bottles do,
From a house you could descry
O'er the garden-wall; is the curtain blue
Or green to a healthy eye?

To mine, it serves for the old June weather
Blue above lane and wall;
And that farthest bottle labelled "Ether"
Is the house o'ertopping all.

At a terrace, somewhere near the stopper,
There watched for me, one June,
A girl: I know, sir, it's improper,
My poor mind's out of tune.

Only, there was a way . . . you crept
Close by the side, to dodge
Eyes in the house, two eyes except:
They styled their house "The Lodge."

What right had a lounger up their lane?
  But, by creeping very close,
With the good wall's help,—their eyes might strain
  And stretch themselves to Oes,

Yet never catch her and me together,
  As she left the attic, there,
By the rim of the bottle labelled "Ether,"
  And stole from stair to stair,

And stood by the rose-wreathed gate. Alas,
  We loved, sir—used to meet:
How sad and bad and mad it was—
  But then, how it was sweet!

May and Death

I WISH that when you died last May,
  Charles, there had died along with you
Three parts of spring's delightful things;
  Ay, and, for me, the fourth part too.

A foolish thought, and worse, perhaps!
  There must be many a pair of friends
Who, arm in arm, deserve the warm
  Moon-births and the long evening-ends.

So, for their sake, be May still May!
  Let their new time, as mine of old;
Do all it did for me: I bid
  Sweet sights and sounds throng manifold.

Only, one little sight, one plant,
  Woods have in May, that starts up green
Save a sole streak which, so to speak,
  Is spring's blood, spilt its leaves between,—

That, they might spare; a certain wood
  Might miss the plant; their loss were small:
But I,—whene'er the leaf grows there,
  Its drop comes from my heart, that's all.

Bifurcation

WE were two lovers; let me lie by her,
My tomb beside her tomb. On hers inscribe—
"I loved him; but my reason bade prefer
Duty to love, reject the tempter's bribe
Of rose and lily when each path diverged,
And either I must pace to life's far end
As love should lead me, or, as duty urged,
Plod the worn causeway arm-in-arm with friend.
So, truth turned falsehood: *'How I loathe a flower,*
How prize the pavement!' still caressed his ear—
The deafish friend's—through life's day, hour by hour,
As he laughed (coughing) *'Ay, it would appear!'*
But deep within my heart of hearts there hid
Ever the confidence, amends for all,
That heaven repairs what wrong earth's journey did,
When love from life-long exile comes at call.
Duty and love, one broad way, were the best—
Who doubts? But one or other was to choose,
I chose the darkling half, and wait the rest
In that new world where light and darkness fuse."

Inscribe on mine—"I loved her: love's track lay
O'er sand and pebble, as all travellers know.
Duty led through a smiling country, gay
With greensward where the rose and lily blow.
'Our roads are diverse: farewell, love!' said she:
''Tis duty I abide by: homely sward
And not the rock-rough picturesque for me!
Above, where both roads join, I wait reward.
Be you as constant to the path whereon

I leave you planted!' But man needs must move,
Keep moving—whither, when the star is gone
Whereby he steps secure nor strays from love?
No stone but I was tripped by, stumbling-block
But brought me to confusion. Where I fell,
There I lay flat, if moss disguised the rock,
Thence, if flint pierced, I rose and cried '*All's well!*
Duty be mine to tread in that high sphere
Where love from duty ne'er disparts, I trust,
And two halves make that whole, whereof—since here
One must suffice a man—why, this one must!' "

Inscribe each tomb thus: then, some sage acquaint
The simple—which holds sinner, which holds saint!

Never the Time and the Place

NEVER the time and the place
  And the loved one all together!
This path—how soft to pace!
  This May—what magic weather!
Where is the loved one's face?
In a dream that loved one's face meets mine,
  But the house is narrow, the place is bleak
Where, outside, rain and wind combine
  With a furtive ear, if I strive to speak,
  With a hostile eye at my flushing cheek,
With a malice that marks each word, each sign!
O enemy sly and serpentine,
  Uncoil thee from the waking man!
    Do I hold the Past
    Thus firm and fast
  Yet doubt if the Future hold I can?
  This path so soft to pace shall lead
  Through the magic of May to herself indeed!
  Or narrow if needs the house must be,
  Outside are the storms and strangers: we—
  Oh, close, safe, warm sleep I and she,
    —I and she!

Passages from "Pauline"

PAULINE, mine own, bend o'er me—thy soft breast
Shall pant to mine—bend o'er me—thy sweet eyes,
And loosened hair and breathing lips, and arms
Drawing me to thee—these build up a screen
To shut me in with thee, and from all fear;
So that I might unlock the sleepless brood
Of fancies from my soul, their lurking-place,
Nor doubt that each would pass, ne'er to return
To one so watched, so loved and so secured.
But what can guard thee but thy naked love?
Ah dearest, whoso sucks a poisoned wound
Envenoms his own veins! Thou art so good,
So calm—if thou shouldst wear a brow less light
For some wild thought which, but for me, were kept
From out thy soul as from a sacred star!
Yet till I have unlocked them it were vain
To hope to sing; some woe would light on me;
Nature would point at one whose quivering lip
Was bathed in her enchantments, whose brow burned
Beneath the crown to which her secrets knelt,
Who learned the spell which can call up the dead,
And then departed smiling like a fiend
Who has deceived God,—if such one should seek
Again her altars and stand robed and crowned
Amid the faithful! Sad confession first,
Remorse and pardon and old claims renewed
Ere I can be—as I shall be no more.
I had been spared this shame if I had sat
By thee forever from the first, in place
Of my wild dreams of beauty and of good,
Or with them, as an earnest of their truth:

No thought nor hope having been shut from thee,
No vague wish unexplained, no wandering aim
Sent back to bind on fancy's wings and seek
Some strange fair world where it might be a law;
But, doubting nothing, had been led by thee,
Through youth, and saved, as one at length awaked
Who has slept through a peril. Ah vain, vain!
Thou lovest me; the past is in its grave
Though its ghost haunts us; still this much is ours,
To cast away restraint, lest a worse thing
Wait for us in the dark. Thou lovest me;
And thou art to receive not love but faith,
For which thou wilt be mine, and smile and take
All shapes and shames, and veil without a fear
That form which music follows like a slave:
And I look to thee and I trust in thee,
As in a Northern night one looks alway
Unto the East for morn and spring and joy.
Thou seest then my aimless, hopeless state,
And, resting on some few old feelings won
Back by thy beauty, wouldst that I essay
The task which was to me what now thou art:
And why should I conceal one weakness more?

Pauline, could I but break the spell! Not now—
All's fever—but when calm shall come again,
I am prepared: I have made life my own.
I would not be content with all the change
One frame should feel, but I have gone in thought
Through all conjuncture, I have lived all life
When it is most alive, where strangest fate

New-shapes it past surmise—the throes of men
Bit by some curse or in the grasps of doom
Half-visible and still-increasing round,
Or crowning their wide being's general aim.

These are wild fancies, but I feel, sweet friend,
As one breathing his weakness to the ear
Of pitying angel—dear as a winter flower,
A slight flower growing alone, and offering
Its frail cup of three leaves to the cold sun,
Yet joyous and confiding like the triumph
Of a child: and why am I not worthy thee?
I can live all the life of plants, and gaze
Drowsily on the bees that flit and play,
Or bare my breast for sunbeams which will kill,
Or open in the night of sounds, to look
For the dim stars; I can mount with the bird
Leaping airily his pyramid of leaves
And twisted boughs of some tall mountain tree
Or rise cheerfully springing to the heavens;
Or like a fish breathe deep the morning air
In the misty sun-warm water; or with flower
And tree can smile in light at the sinking sun
Just as the storm comes, as a girl would look
On a departing lover—most serene.

Pauline, come with me, see how I could build
A home for us, out of the world, in thought!
I am uplifted: fly with me, Pauline!

Lyrics from "Ferishtah's Fancies"

1

ROUND us the wild creatures, overhead the trees,
Underfoot the moss-tracks,—life and love with these!
I to wear a fawn-skin, thou to dress in flowers:
All the long lone summer-day, that greenwood life of ours!

Rich-pavilioned, rather,—still the world without,—
Inside—gold-roofed silk-walled silence round about!
Queen it thou on purple,—I, at watch, and ward
Couched beneath the columns, gaze, thy slave, love's guard!

So, for us no world? Let throngs press thee to me!
Up and down amid men, heart by heart fare we!
Welcome squalid vesture, harsh voice, hateful face!
God is soul, souls I and thou: with souls should souls have
place.

2

Wish no word unspoken, want no look away!
What if words were but mistake, and looks—too sudden,
say!
Be unjust for once, Love! Bear it—well I may!

Do me justice always? Bid my heart—their shrine—
Render back its store of gifts, old looks and words of thine
—Oh, so all unjust—the less deserved, the more divine?

3

You groped your way across my room i' the drear dark dead of night;
At each fresh step a stumble was: but, once your lamp alight,
Easy and plain you walked again: so soon all wrong grew right!

What lay on floor to trip your foot? Each object, late awry,
Looked fitly placed, nor proved offence to footing free—for why?
The lamp showed all, discordant late, grown simple symmetry.

Be love your light and trust your guide, with these explore my heart!
No obstacle to trip you then, strike hands and souls apart!
Since rooms and hearts are furnished so,—light shows you,—needs love start?

4

Man I am and man would be, Love—merest man and nothing more.
Bid me seem no other! Eagles boast of pinions—let them soar!
I may put forth angel's plumage, once unmanned, but not before.

Now on earth, to stand suffices,—nay, if kneeling serves, to kneel:
Here you front me, here I find the all of heaven that earth can feel:
Sense looks straight,—not over, under,—perfect sees beyond appeal.

Good you are and wise, full circle: what to me were more outside?
Wiser wisdom, better goodness? Ah, such want the angel's wide
Sense to take and hold and keep them! Mine at least has never tried.

5

So, the head aches and the limbs are faint!
  Flesh is a burden—even to you!
Can I force a smile with a fancy quaint?
  Why are my ailments none or few?

In the soul of me sits sluggishness:
  Body so strong and will so weak:
The slave stands fit for the labor—yes,
  But the master's mandate is still to seek.

You, now—what if the outside clay
  Helped, not hindered the inside flame?
My dim to-morrow—your plain to-day,
  Yours the achievement, mine the aim?

So were it rightly, so shall it be!
  Only, while earth we pace together
For the purpose apportioned you and me,
  Closer we tread for a common tether.

You shall sigh, "Wait for his sluggish soul!
  Shame he should lag, not lamed as I!"
May not I smile, "Ungained her goal:
  Body may reach her—by and by?"

6

Verse-making was least of my virtues: I viewed with despair
Wealth that never yet was but might be—all that verse-making were
If the life would but lengthen to wish, let the mind be laid bare.
So I said "To do little is bad, to do nothing is worse"—
        And made verse.

Love-making,—how simple a matter! No depths to explore,
No heights in a life to ascend! No disheartening Before,
No affrighting Hereafter,—love now will be love evermore.
So I felt "To keep silence were folly:"—all language above,
        I made love.

7

Not with my Soul, Love!—bid no soul like mine
  Lap thee around nor leave the poor Sense room!
Soul,—travel-worn, toil-weary,—would confine
  Along with Soul, Soul's gains from glow and gloom,

Captures from soarings high and divings deep.
Spoil-laden Soul, how should such memories sleep?
  Take Sense, too—let me love entire and whole—
    Not with my Soul!

Eyes shall meet eyes and find no eyes between,
  Lips feed on lips, no other lips to fear!
No past, no future—so thine arms but screen
  The present from surprise! not there, 'tis here—
Not then, 'tis now:—back, memories that intrude!
Make, Love, the universe our solitude,
  And, over all the rest, oblivion roll—
    Sense quenching Soul!

8

Ask not one least word of praise!
  Words declare your eyes are bright?
What then meant that summer day's
Silence spent in one long gaze?
  Was my silence wrong or right?

Words of praise were all to seek!
  Face of you and form of you.
Did they find the praise so weak
When my lips just touched your cheek—
  Touch which let my soul come through?

From "Fifine at the Fair"

YOUR husband holds you fast,
Will have you listen, learn your character at last!
"Do I say?—like her mixed unrest and discontent,
Reproachfulness and scorn, with that submission blent
So strangely, in the face, by sad smiles and gay tears,—
Quiescence which attacks, rebellion which endears,—
Say? 'As you loved me once, could you but love me now!
Years probably have graved their passage on my brow,
Lips turn more rarely red, eyes sparkle less than erst;
Such tribute body pays to time; but, unamerced,
The soul retains, nay, boasts old treasure multiplied.
Though dew-prime flee,—mature at noonday, love defied
Chance, the wind, change, the rain: love strenuous all the more
For storm, struck deeper root and choicer fruitage bore,
Despite the rocking world; yet truth struck root in vain:
While tenderness bears fruit, you praise, not taste again.
Why? They are yours, which once were hardly yours, might go
To grace another's ground: and then—the hopes we know,
The fears we keep in mind!—when, ours to arbitrate,
Your part was to bow neck, bid fall decree of fate.
Then, O the knotty point—white-night's work to revolve—
What meant that smile, that sigh? Not Solon's self could solve!
Then, O the deep surmise what one word might express,
And if what seemed her "No" may not have meant her "Yes!"
Then, such annoy, for cause—calm welcome, such acquist
Of rapture if, refused her arm, hand touched her wrist!
Now, what's a smile to you? Poor candle that lights up

The decent household gloom which sends you out to sup.
A tear? worse! warns that health requires you keep aloof
From nuptial chamber, since rain penetrates the roof!
Soul, body got and gained, inalienably safe
Your own, become despised; more worth has any waif
Or stray from neighbor's pale: pouch that,—'tis pleasure, pride,
Novelty, property, and larceny beside!
Preposterous thought! to find no value fixed in things,
To covet all you see, hear, dream of, till fate brings
About that, what you want, you gain; then follows change.
Give you the sun to keep, forthwith must fancy range:
A goodly lamp, no doubt,—yet might you catch her hair
And capture, as she frisks, the fen-fire dancing there!
What do I say? at least a meteor's half in heaven;
Provided filth but shine, my husband hankers even
After putridity that's phosphorescent, cribs
The rustic's tallow-rush, makes spoil of urchins' squibs,
In short, prefers to me—chaste, temperate, serene—
What sputters green and blue, this fizgig called Fifine!' "

From "Numpholeptos"

STILL you stand, still you listen, still you smile!
Still melts your moonbeam through me, white awhile,
Softening, sweetening, till sweet and soft
Increase so round this heart of mine, that oft
I could believe your moonbeam-smile has past
The pallid limit, lies, transformed at last
To sunlight and salvation—warms the soul
It sweetens, softens! Would you pass that goal,
Gain love's birth at the limit's happier verge,
And, where an iridescence lurks, but urge
The hesitating pallor on to prime
Of dawn! true blood-streaked, sun-warmth, action-time,
By heart-pulse ripened to a ruddy glow
Of gold above my clay—I scarce should know
From gold's self, thus suffused! For gold means love.
What means the sad slow silver smile above
My clay but pity, pardon?—at the best,
But acquiescence that I take my rest,
Contented to be clay, while in your heaven
The sun reserves love for the Spirit-Seven
Companioning God's throne they lamp before,
—Leaves earth a mute waste only wandered o'er
By that pale soft sweet disempassioned moon
Which smiles me slow forgiveness! Such, the boon
I beg? Nay, dear, submit to this—just this
Supreme endeavor! As my lips now kiss
Your feet, my arms convulse your shrouding robe,
My eyes acquainted with the dust, dare probe
Your eyes above for—what, if born would blind
Mine with redundant bliss, as flash may find

The inert nerve, sting awake the palsied limb,
Bid with life's ecstasy sense overbrim
And suck back death in the resurging joy—
Love, the love whole and sole without alloy!

A Face

IF one could have that little head of hers
  Painted upon a background of pale gold,
Such as the Tuscan's early art prefers!
  No shade encroaching on the matchless mould
Of those two lips, which should be opening soft
  In the pure profile; not as when she laughs,
For that spoils all: but rather as if aloft
  Yon hyacinth, she loves so, leaned its staff's
Burthen of honey-coloured buds to kiss
And capture 'twixt the lips apart for this.
Then her lithe neck, three fingers might surround,
How it should waver on the pale gold ground
Up to the fruit-shaped, perfect chin it lifts!
I know, Correggio loves to mass, in rifts
Of heaven, his angel faces, orb on orb
Breaking its outline, burning shades absorb:
But these are only massed there, I should think,
  Waiting to see some wonder momently
  Grow out, stand full, fade slow against the sky
  (That's the pale ground you'd see this sweet face by),
  All heaven, meanwhile, condensed into one eye
Which fears to lose the wonder, should it wink.

One Word More

TO E. B. B.

I

THERE they are, my fifty men and women
Naming me the fifty poems finished!
Take them, Love, the book and me together;
Where the heart lies, let the brain lie also.

II

Rafael made a century of sonnets,
Made and wrote them in a certain volume
Dinted with the silver-pointed pencil
Else he only used to draw Madonnas:
These, the world might view—but one, the volume.
Who that one, you ask? Your heart instructs you.
Did she live and love it all her lifetime?
Did she drop, his lady of the sonnets,
Die, and let it drop beside her pillow
Where it lay in place of Rafael's glory,
Rafael's cheek so duteous and so loving—
Cheek, the world was wont to hail a painter's,
Rafael's cheek, her love had turned a poet's?

III

You and I would rather read that volume,
(Taken to his beating bosom by it)
Lean and list the bosom-beats of Rafael,
Would we not? than wonder at Madonnas—
Her, San Sisto names, and Her, Foligno,
Her, that visits Florence in a vision,
Her, that's left with lilies in the Louvre—
Seen by us and all the world in circle.

IV

You and I will never read that volume.
Guido Reni, like his own eye's apple
Guarded long the treasure-book and loved it.
Guido Reni dying, all Bologna
Cried, and the world cried too, "Ours, the treasure!"
Suddenly, as rare things will, it vanished.

V

Dante once prepared to paint an angel:
Whom to please? You whisper "Beatrice."
While he mused and traced it and retraced it,
(Peradventure with a pen corroded
Still by drops of that hot ink he dipped for,
When, his left-hand i' the hair o' the wicked,
Back he held the brow and pricked its stigma,
Bit into the live man's flesh for parchment,
Loosed him, laughed to see the writing rankle,
Let the wretch go festering through Florence) –
Dante, who loved well because he hated,
Hated wickedness that hinders loving,
Dante standing, studying his angel, –
In there broke the folk of his Inferno.
Says he – "Certain people of importance"
(Such he gave his daily dreadful line to)
"Entered and would seize, forsooth, the poet."
Says the poet – "Then I stopped my painting."

VI

You and I would rather see that angel,
Painted by the tenderness of Dante,
Would we not? – than read a fresh Inferno.

VII

You and I will never see that picture.
While he mused on love and Beatrice,
While he softened o'er his outlined angel,
In they broke, those "people of importance:"
We and Bice bear the loss forever.

VIII

What of Rafael's sonnets, Dante's picture?
This: no artist lives and loves, that longs not
Once, and only once, and for one only,
(Ah, the prize!) to find his love a language
Fit and fair and simple and sufficient—
Using nature that's an art to others,
Not, this one time, art that's turned his nature.
Ay, of all the artists living, loving,
None but would forgo his proper dowry,—
Does he paint? he fain would write a poem,—
Does he write? he fain would paint a picture,
Put to proof art alien to the artist's,
Once, and only once, and for one only,
So to be the man and leave the artist,
Gain the man's joy, miss the artist's sorrow.

IX

Wherefore? Heaven's gift takes earth's abatement!
He who smites the rock and spreads the water,
Bidding drink and live a crowd beneath him,
Even he, the minute makes immortal,
Proves, perchance, but mortal in the minute,
Desecrates, belike, the deed in doing.
While he smites, how can he but remember,

So he smote before, in such a peril,
When they stood and mocked—"Shall smiting help us?"
When they drank and sneered—"A stroke is easy!"
When they wiped their mouths and went their journey,
Throwing him for thanks—"But drought was pleasant."
Thus old memories mar the actual triumph;
Thus the doing savors of disrelish;
Thus achievement lacks a gracious somewhat;
O'er-importuned brows becloud the mandate,
Carelessness or consciousness—the gesture.
For he bears an ancient wrong about him,
Sees and knows again those phalanxed faces,
Hears, yet one time more, the 'customed prelude—
"How shouldst thou, of all men, smite, and save us?"
Guesses what is like to prove the sequel—
"Egypt's flesh-pots—nay, the drought was better."

X

Oh, the crowd must have emphatic warrant!
Theirs, the Sinai-forehead's cloven brilliance,
Right-arm's rod-sweep, tongue's imperial fiat.
Never dares the man put off the prophet.

XI

Did he love one face from out the thousands,
(Were she Jethro's daughter, white and wifely,
Were she but the Æthiopian bondslave,)
He would envy yon dumb patient camel,
Keeping a reserve of scanty water
Meant to save his own life in the desert;
Ready in the desert to deliver
(Kneeling down to let his breast be opened)
Hoard and life together for his mistress.

XII

I shall never, in the years remaining,
Paint you pictures, no, nor carve you statues,
Make you music that should all-express me;
So it seems: I stand on my attainment.
This of verse alone, one life allows me;
Verse and nothing else have I to give you.
Other heights in other lives, God willing:
All the gifts from all the heights, your own, Love!

XIII

Yet a semblance of resource avails us—
Shade so finely touched, love's sense must seize it.
Take these lines, look lovingly and nearly,
Lines I write the first time and the last time.
He who works in fresco, steals a hair-brush,
Curbs the liberal hand, subservient proudly,
Cramps his spirit, crowds its all in little,
Makes a strange art of an art familiar,
Fills his lady's missal-marge with flowerets.
He who blows through bronze, may breathe through silver,
Fitly serenade a slumbrous princess.
He who writes, may write for once as I do.

XIV

Love, you saw me gather men and women,
Live or dead or fashioned by my fancy,
Enter each and all, and use their service,
Speak from every mouth,—the speech, a poem.
Hardly shall I tell my joys and sorrows,
Hopes and fears, belief and disbelieving:
I am mine and yours—the rest be all men's,

Karshish, Cleon, Norbert, and the fifty.
Let me speak this once in my true person,
Not as Lippo, Roland, or Andrea,
Though the fruit of speech be just this sentence:
Pray you, look on these my men and women,
Take and keep my fifty poems finished;
Where my heart lies, let my brain lie also!
Poor the speech; be how I speak, for all things.

XV

Not but that you know me! Lo, the moon's self!
Here in London, yonder late in Florence,
Still we find her face, the thrice-transfigured.
Curving on a sky imbrued with color,
Drifted over Fiesole by twilight,
Came she, our new crescent of a hair's-breadth.
Full she flared it, lamping Samminiato,
Rounder 'twixt the cypresses and rounder,
Perfect till the nightingales applauded.
Now, a piece of her old self, impoverished,
Hard to greet, she traverses the house-roofs,
Hurries with unhandsome thrift of silver,
Goes dispiritedly, glad to finish.

XVI

What, there's nothing in the moon noteworthy?
Nay: for if that moon could love a mortal,
Use, to charm him (so to fit a fancy),
All her magic ('tis the old sweet mythos),
She would turn a new side to her mortal,
Side unseen of herdsman, huntsman, steersman—
Blank to Zoroaster on his terrace,
Blind to Galileo on his turret,

Dumb to Homer, dumb to Keats—him, even!
Think, the wonder of the moonstruck mortal—
When she turns round, comes again in heaven,
Opens out anew for worse or better!
Proves she like some portent of an iceberg
Swimming full upon the ship it founders,
Hungry with huge teeth of splintered crystals?
Proves she as the paved work of a sapphire
Seen by Moses when he climbed the mountain?
Moses, Aaron, Nadab and Abihu
Climbed and saw the very God, the Highest,
Stand upon the paved work of a sapphire.
Like the bodied heaven in his clearness
Shone the stone, the sapphire of that paved work,
When they ate and drank and saw God also!

XVII

What were seen? None knows, none ever shall know.
Only this is sure—the sight were other,
Not the moon's same side, born late in Florence,
Dying now impoverished here in London.
God be thanked, the meanest of his creatures
Boasts two soul-sides, one to face the world with,
One to show a woman when he loves her!

XVIII

This I say of me, but think of you, Love!
This to you—yourself my moon of poets!
Ah, but that's the world's side, there's the wonder,
Thus they see you, praise you, think they know you!
There, in turn I stand with them and praise you—
Out of my own self, I dare to phrase it.
But the best is when I glide from out them,

Cross a step or two of dubious twilight,
Come out on the other side, the novel
Silent silver lights and darks undreamed of,
Where I hush and bless myself with silence.

XIX

Oh, their Rafael of the dear Madonnas,
Oh, their Dante of the dread Inferno,
Wrote one song—and in my brain I sing it,
Drew one angel—borne, see, on my bosom!

R. B.

(Originally appended to *Men and Women*)